The Euro-American Cinema

T0339322

TEXAS FILM STUDIES SERIES

Thomas Schatz, Editor

THE EURO-AMERICAN CINEMA
Peter Lev

 University of Texas Press, Austin

First edition, 1993

Requests for permission to reproduce material
from this work should be sent to
Permissions, University of Texas Press,
Box 7819, Austin, TX 78713-7819.
utpress.utexas.edu/index.php/rp-form
LIBRARY OF CONGRESS
CATALOGING-IN-PUBLICATION DATA

Lev, Peter, date
   The Euro-American cinema / Peter Lev. – 1st ed.
      p.   cm. — (Texas film studies series)
   Filmography: p.
   Includes bibliographical references (p.   ) and index.
   ISBN 0-292-74677-6 (cloth). — ISBN 0-292-74678-4 (pbk.)
   1. Motion pictures—Europe. 2. Motion pictures—
International cooperation. I. Title. II. Series.
PN1993.5.E8L48   1993
791.43'094—dc20   92-42794

Design and typography by George Lenox

ISBN 978-0-292-74678-7

FOR HERBERT AND YOLA LEV

Contents

Acknowledgments

I owe thanks to a number of individuals and institutions for generously helping me in the preparation of this book.

In Los Angeles: Stephen Mamber, Mark and Patricia Treadwell, Don and Sue Silver, Richard and Jan Miller, Burt Senkfor, Sam Gill, and the libraries of UCLA, USC, and the Academy of Motion Picture Arts and Sciences.

In New York: Mary Corliss, Museum of Modern Art/Film Stills Archive, Performing Arts Research Center of New York Public Library.

In Madison, Wisconsin: Tino Balio, Harry Miller, Wisconsin Center for Film and Theater Research.

In Bozeman, Montana: Paul Monaco.

In Washington, D.C.: Library of Congress.

In Maryland: Sheryl Williams, Beverly Lorenz, Kosta Kostadinov, Greg Faller, Barry Moore, Steve Weiss, Maria Saccone, Bill Horne, Ron Matlon, Gloria Gaguski, Gilbert Brungardt, Annette Chappell, Gary Edgerton, Bob Kolker, Video Americain, Marcella Fultz, Susan Mower, Marc Sober, Roger Lewin, Joan Lewin, Yvonne Lev, Sara Lev, and the libraries of Towson State University, Johns Hopkins University, University of Maryland Baltimore County, University of Maryland College Park, and Enoch Pratt Free Library.

Special thanks to Provost Robert Caret, Dean Esslinger, and the Faculty Research and Faculty Development Committees of Towson State University for their financial support of my research.

Special thanks as well to my editors, Tom Schatz of the University of Texas and Frankie Westbrook of U.T. Press.

An earlier version of Chapter 6, "Art and Commerce in *Contempt*," appeared in *New Orleans Review* 15, no. 3 (Fall, 1988). Reprinted by permission of the *New Orleans Review*, © 1988. An earlier version of Chapter 7, "*Blow-Up*, Swinging London, and the Film Generation," was originally published by *Literature/Film Quarterly*, Vol. 17, No. 2, © Salisbury State University, Md. (1989). Reprinted by permission.

Introduction

Since World War II, the film production industries of the United States and Western Europe have become thoroughly intertwined. Many prestigious European films are co-productions involving two or more European countries plus financial participation of an American distributor. Most of the best-known European directors have made English-language films—Antonioni, Bertolucci, Bergman, Costa-Gavras, De Sica, Fassbinder, Godard, Malle, Rossellini, Tavernier, Truffaut, Visconti, and Wenders are some of the names which come to mind. American stars such as Burt Lancaster, Jane Fonda, Jack Nicholson, and Robert de Niro have made European films, in English or other languages. European stars ranging from Sophia Loren and Gina Lollobrigida in the 1950s to Rutger Hauer and Isabelle Adjani in the 1980s have been prominently featured in American films. "A number of recent major films have had no nationality in a meaningful sense at all," wrote critic Geoffrey Nowell-Smith in 1985.[1] Sometimes a film's nationality changes according to the distributor's convenience or legal advantage. A high-budget American film shot in part on British sound stages may be "British" for the purpose of obtaining a government subsidy, and an Italian-Spanish English-language production filmed in Spain with American money may be "Italian" in Italy for similar reasons. The question of nationality has become so problematic that in 1988 both the Cannes and the Venice Film Festivals dispensed with national labels and listed films by the director's last name.[2]

This new internationalism should not be conceptualized as a neutral, cosmopolitan arrangement among equal partners. It should be seen, rather, as an unequal partnership between large American film companies with global operations and European filmmakers and governments struggling to maintain national film industries. The American film industry has dominated the export of motion pictures on a world scale since World War I. Although American market share in Europe has fluctuated widely since 1945, with high points around 1950 and in the late 1980s, the United States has consistently been the leading exporter of films to Western Europe. Even in the major European film-producing nations—France, Italy, Great Britain, West Germany—the American share of the film market has often surpassed the local film industry's share. Further, American companies began investing on a large scale in European film production about 1960, so that British, French, or Italian films may be largely American-financed. American financial participation means that the needs of the American market must be considered in writing, casting, shooting, and editing a film.

This study examines one type of film that clearly demonstrates the influence of the American film industry on European film production in the post–World War II period: the big-budget English-language film made by a European art film director. I call this type of film the "Euro-American art film." It attempts a synthesis of the American entertainment film (large budget, good production values, internationally known stars) and the European art film (auteur director, artistic subject and/or style) with the aim of reaching a much larger audience than the art film normally commands. Some well-known examples are *Blow-Up* (1966), *Last Tango in Paris* (1972), *Paris, Texas* (1984), and *The Last Emperor* (1987).

I have two main reasons for focusing on the art film. First, the art film has been the most internationally successful and prestigious type of film made in Europe in the post–World War II period. David Bordwell describes it as the first important challenge and alternative to the Hollywood classical style of feature filmmaking.[3] The encounter between the European art film and the Hollywood companies active in Europe is therefore a key moment in film history. Second, the emphasis on the Euro-American art film allows me to talk about the intersection of American and European filmmaking in relation to a number of excellent films. *Paisan, Voyage to Italy, Never on Sunday, Contempt, Blow-Up, Fahrenheit 451, Last Tango in Paris, The Passenger, 1900, The American Friend, Paris, Texas, The Last Emperor,* and *Bagdad Cafe* are major films which show the influence of European-American collaboration in their content and structure. The concentration on these films, rather than on a more conventional genre cinema, leads to a discussion that is qualitative and aesthetic as well as quantitative.

My study does not pretend to be a complete history of the growing together of American and European film industries. It follows one line of development: the history of the European art film from strictly national productions to Euro-American, between-cultures films. The growing American economic presence in European film industries of the 1950s and 1960s is discussed as an essential contributing element to the Euro-American art film. However, little attention is paid to the European-made Hollywood spectaculars circa 1960 (*Ben Hur, El Cid, Cleopatra*), to the Spaghetti Westerns circa 1965, or to the problems of smaller film-producing countries such as Belgium, the Netherlands, and Sweden. The special status of the British cinema, which derives economic gain but also a loss of cultural autonomy from a very close association with the Hollywood film industry, is discussed in passing rather than isolated as a major topic for analysis. This book looks primarily at films involving collaborations between American companies and French or Italian filmmakers, France and Italy being the two most prominent film-producing countries in Western Europe.

The term "culture" is used here in two interrelated senses. First, culture is the way of life of a group of people, the pattern of work, play, tradition, belief, family structure, and so on. Second, more narrowly, culture can be defined as the range of intellectual and artistic activities which provide meaning and identity for a particular group.[4] I emphasize the second definition, but treat it as a special case of the first, very broad definition. Elaborating on the second definition, culture would include both the traditional arts and humanities—painting, music, literature, philosophy, history—and the popular arts and mass media.[5] Culture encompasses the artifacts themselves (books, records, films) and the institutions which produce and distribute them. Culture can have a national focus, but it can also refer to a transnational unit (European culture), or to an ethnic, class, or regional group. My central focus involves the place of film—artifacts plus institutions—in the cultures of Western Europe and the United States. A cultural distinction between Western Europe and the United States could be challenged, since these two areas have a great deal in common in terms of intellectual and artistic heritage. Cultural differences between Europe and East Asia, to take just one example, are much more pronounced. However, in looking at film in the context of West European and American societies, both the artifacts produced and the institutions of production and reception are significantly different in the two cases. Even the status of film—high art or popular art?—in the overall culture varies, with European critics, audiences, and government agencies more likely than their American counterparts to consider film a high art. Therefore, the attempt to make films with a combination of American and European methods and personnel, and to meet the expectations of both a popular entertainment and an art-film audience, can be seen as a "cross-cultural" or "between-cultures" endeavor.

What are the consequences of making cultural products that are neither American nor European, but something in between? Film historian Thomas Guback stresses the threat to cultural autonomy represented by American participation in European film industries. For Guback, American financial backing may be desirable in a short-term economic sense, but in the long term it endangers the stability and the cultural identity of local film industries.[6] However, whereas Guback has concentrated on the economic backdrop of American-European interactions in recent film history, my study tries to combine economic data with the history and criticism of the films produced as American and European film industries collided and in some ways merged. From this perspective, the notion of American economic and cultural domination presented by Guback needs to be modified to suggest a more complex and subtle relationship. For if the last forty years do show a strong American presence and influence in European film industries, they also show significant European influences on American film. An overall movement toward greater American control—toward an English-language film industry with no significant European competition—is countered by European efforts to create an economically and culturally viable cinema. At times these two goals meet in the fascinating, hybrid films I have labeled "Euro-American art films."

The methodology used in this book is eclectic. I employ Antonio Gramsci's concept of hegemony (dominance by cultural adherence) to describe the American influence on European films. Hegemony is a more useful term than cultural imperialism, which confuses domination by economic and political force with domination by culture. In Gramsci's terms, American cultural hegemony over European film industries is achieved through attractive, popular elements as well as through economic advantages. But the hegemony of a dominant group is a complex and ever-changing cultural process which can be challenged and modified under certain historical conditions by the culture of subordinate groups. This is what happens in the interaction of American and European film industries, where in moments of crisis and loss of confidence in the American film industry, and in American society, European film has influenced the usually dominant American film industry. To a Gramscian model of cross-cultural influence I add economic analysis, which shows how economic factors channel the kinds of films that are made; production history, which shows the interaction of European and American filmmaking in specific film projects and at specific historical moments; and close readings of individual films, with particular attention to the perspectives and contexts suggested by the other methods of analysis.

There is also an auteurist perspective to my book. Art-film directors often work from an aesthetic theory of artistic self-expression. Art-film critics and audiences, working from the same theory, typically value the formal and narrative characteristics associated with a particular director's work. The art film is primarily a director's medium, and for art-entertainment hybrids the director's "style" (image, sound, narrative) is one component of the synthesis. In this study I recognize the privileging of the director by the art film; but I add an awareness of the limitations of the auteur theory (director as author) as a description of film history. Via economic analysis, production history, and discussions of genre, period, and subject matter I try to go beyond a simple identification of the director as creator of a film.

This book is divided into two parts. Part one presents my historical and theoretical argument on the development and significance of the Euro-American art film. Specific chapters cover the art film, the increasing American participation in European film industries, and the Euro-American art film. Part two is devoted to case studies of individual films. The two-part structure reflects my belief that film history must involve a dynamic interplay between historical overview and detailed film analysis. To paraphrase Andrew Sarris, the subject matter of film history is both "the forest" and "the trees."[7]

The Euro-American Cinema

Part I: History and Theory

OPEN CITY
Images of resistance, images of decadence.

1. The Art Film

The term "art" is so problematic that some textbooks on the subject avoid defining it. Nevertheless, I will sketch out some elements of a definition. "Art" refers to a human-produced object, text, or performance which has limited immediate utility (a sculpture is not a coat rack), but several layers of "extra" meaning or value. Most prominent of these extra layers are beauty, affective power, and social meaning or insight. The social meaning of a work of art often focuses on the most mysterious aspects of a culture, for example religion or romantic love. But this social meaning can also be simple and direct, as in the "agit-prop" emphasis of much Soviet art. In the Western world, art is separated from the non-artistic by a history of hundreds of years, and by institutions—artists, critics, schools, museums, performance centers—which promote and sustain the arts.

These same institutions distinguish between "high art" and "popular art," or "art" and "entertainment" (the two sets of terms are more or less equivalent). High art assumes a sophisticated public with much previous exposure to the arts, and with extensive knowledge of artistic conventions. This type of art is a serious matter, appealing to thought as well as emotion. Popular art, or entertainment, has its own set of conventions but is easily accessible to a broad audience. Popular art is emotionally direct: it makes people laugh, cry, have a good time. Customarily, high art or "fine art" has included painting, sculpture, literature, theater, music, and dance. Film has generally been considered a popular art, though some critics have contested the meaningfulness of this distinction. However, certain types of film have been produced and viewed within the traditions and expectations of high art.

The desire to make films for artistic appreciation, and not solely for profit, has been a continuing impulse in film history. The Film d'Art of 1912, the Russian, German, and French avant-gardes of the 1920s, and the early sound films of Buñuel, Cocteau, and Vigo are all examples of films self-consciously situated within high art traditions. The Film d'Art drew on classical theater, the German avant-garde on Expressionism, the

films of Buñuel on Surrealism. However, the term "art film" refers specifically to feature films made in the post–World War II period (and continuing to the present) which display new ideas of form and content and
which are aimed at a high-culture audience. Most of these films were
made in Europe, and the most significant European film movements of
the past forty years (Italian neorealism, French New Wave, Czech New
Wave, New German Cinema) may all be seen as part of the "art film"
phenomenon.

Only a few attempts have been made to define the art film. To
some extent, definitions have been made by spectators and exhibitors.
"Art theaters" serving a somewhat different public from commercial
theaters began in a few world capitals in the 1920s,[1] and by the late
1940s art-film theaters had become an established part of film exhibition. At the risk of tautology, one could say that art films are what is
shown in art theaters.

David Bordwell and Steve Neale have attempted more rigorous
definitions. In Bordwell's formalist analysis, the art film is marked by a
concentration on character, an attenuation of cause-effect logic, and an
increased emphasis on realism and authorial expressivity.[2] For viewers,
the key attribute of the art film is ambiguity—the spectator must
choose whether to interpret breaks in classical (Hollywood) film style
as moving toward greater realism or authorial comment, or both. In
many art films, says Bordwell, ambiguous material is open to interpretations "suggesting character subjectivity, life's untidyness, and author's vision."[3] This openness links the art film to modern schools of
literature and painting, and it is arguably more true to human experience than the linear cause-effect narratives of Hollywood. Bordwell's
definition is important as the first attempt to go beyond thoroughly subjective notions of the "art" of the art film. However, his formalist emphasis does not provide an adequate basis for a social-historical, rather
than strictly aesthetic, account of the art film.

Steve Neale presents a "textual" definition of the art film similar
to Bordwell's, but adds a useful institutional definition.[4] Neale's textual
definition describes a stress on character and visual style, a suppression
of action, and an interiorization of dramatic conflicts as key features of
the art film. In his institutional analysis, Neale defines the two goals of
the art film: to counter American domination of European local markets, and to support local film industries and film cultures. In an attempt to reach these goals, the art film is differentiated from Hollywood
commercial cinema and attached to high art and culture. This creates
an opportunity for art films to establish their own cultural and economic niche. Neale notes that European art films are supported by a

network of institutions, including government-subsidized production, film festivals, specialized journals, and art theaters. They are also supported by the discourses of art and culture within a particular country. Although the films themselves may be quite diverse, following a theory of individualized artistic creation, "they tend to be unified and stabilized" by the institutional framework.[5]

One element which Neale surprisingly omits is that the art film is intended for an *international* audience. Its marketing strategy depends on reaching a relatively small, culturally elite audience in several countries, rather than serving the local market alone. A low- to medium-budget film can make a reasonable profit if it reaches art theater audiences in Western Europe, the United States, and Canada. These audiences are not well-served by Hollywood films, so the art film can be seen as a kind of counter-programming. Some of the art film institutions Neale describes (film festivals, government subsidies) are specifically aimed at encouraging export. And, in addition to obvious economic benefits, the export of artistic films also provides cultural prestige.

A further international aspect of the art film is that it assumes a cosmopolitan, non-chauvinist spectator who can empathize with characters from many nations. Subtitling, not dubbing, is standard for the art film, and this requires a spectator who is tolerant of other languages and other cultures. Although art films are not automatically in foreign languages (anything but English, for an American audience), the art film spectator is expected to accept intercultural, as well as intracultural, communications. The intercultural communication is usually European in origin, which connects the art film to other high-culture pursuits (e.g., classical music, opera).

Dudley Andrew, in *Film in the Aura of Art*, provides an alternative to the Bordwell and Neale definitions of the art film, saying that art films are precisely those which insist on being surprising and unique, outside of any standardized textual system. For Andrew, the identification of an art film depends on the individual spectator; this justifies the somewhat surprising choice of *Meet John Doe* as an art film in his book. But individual choices are channeled by the films available for viewing and by the possible interpretations within a society at a particular time. For Andrew, institutional and historical factors influence, but do not entirely determine, individual choice. With Andrew's ideas, we can make more sense of the notion that art films are what is shown in art theaters. The repertoire of films that plays in art theaters is determined by viewer choices; exhibitor, distributor, and producer choices; the influence of art film institutions (e.g., festivals); and the range of possible interpretations of film at a particular time.[6]

Combining the Bordwell, Neale, and Andrew definitions, we can say that the art film as a category is pulled toward standardization by the need of the viewer for a relatively stable system of interpretation and by the unifying institutional network; yet it is also pulled toward diversity by the idea of art as something new, unique, surprising. The art film's "space" is defined by this tension. The notion of the art film will never be entirely stable, but will be created by the tension between standardization and diversity, as worked out in specific historical circumstances.

The history of the art film has not yet been written. One large barrier to such a history is that the art film is both an international phenomenon and one which depends on local exhibition history. A complete history of the art film would include films from Western Europe, Eastern Europe, the United States, Canada, Japan, India, and perhaps Latin America and Africa.[7] Given this range of producing countries, an internationalist perspective seems called for. Yet the history of the art film also depends very much on the exhibition perspective of individual countries: What films were exhibited? What films were widely discussed? What institutional structures aided and shaped the art film? In the United States, for example, the art film has been promoted mainly by small distributors and exhibitors, as well as by critics, and all definitions of the "art film" and the "art theater" are approximate. In France, on the other hand, the Ministry of Culture has joined with private enterprise to promote and encourage the art film by providing tax breaks and other forms of subsidy. In doing so, the government has had to write official definitions of what constitutes a "cinéma d'art et essai" and a "film d'art et essai," and to interpret these definitions on a yearly basis.[8] In England, to give a third example, privately owned art-film theaters spread throughout the country have gradually been replaced by government-supported art theaters and regional media centers. Distribution of artistic and cultural films has also, to a large extent, been taken over by the government. This means that public institutions such as the British Film Institute, rather than the interplay of distributors and exhibitors, decide which films will be distributed.[9] Clearly, the history of the art film in Britain or France centrally involves public institutions, whereas in the United States private enterprise has controlled distribution and exhibition.

Local perspectives on the art film may also vary greatly in terms of the importance of individual films and filmmakers. For example, Pier Paolo Pasolini was a tremendously important filmmaker, and theorist, and personality, in Italy until his death in 1975. In the United States, Pasolini's films have received little or no distribution, and he is not a widely known figure.[10] Lina Wertmuller, on the other hand, is more respected in the United States than she is in Italy. Nevertheless, there does seem to be a common core of agreement in the United States and Western Europe on the importance of certain film movements (neorealism, the French New Wave, the New German Cinema) and certain directors (Fellini, Antonioni, Godard, Bergman, Fassbinder).

In this study, the perspective taken on the art film will inevitably have an American slant, since the author is American and has spent twenty-five years viewing and thinking about art films in an American context. The American viewpoint is significant, since the United States is by far the single largest market for motion pictures in the world, and the commercial success or failure of art films often depends on their reception in the United States. However, the American viewpoint is mainly one of reception (critical reception, academic reception, audience reception), and it must be balanced by the European context of art-film production. This is one of the virtues of Steve Neale's work, which presents the art film as (among other things) a production strategy, and thinks through the benefits and problems of such a strategy. So, in my history of the art film, and in other parts of this study, Western European perspectives will be prominently featured, especially in terms of art-film production. The goal is to present the art film not only as a certain type of cinematic artifact, but also as a relationship between production and reception, and as a phenomenon with both international and national dimensions.

HISTORY

My presentation of the art film begins at the close of World War II, and thus omits such distinguished moments in film history as German Expressionism and the Russian montage school. Within this framework, the key event which begins the art film's history is Italian neorealism, which demonstrated that low-budget, artistically ambitious films could reach international audiences. Neorealist films can be characterized as fiction films about the present or immediate past, showing the actual living conditions of poor people, and shot with such documentary or semi-documentary conventions as on-location filming and the use of non-professional actors. Neorealist films concentrated on character and social environment rather than plot, and made a drastic break with the cinema of glamor and luxury.

Why were international audiences excited about the unglamorous images and sounds of Italian neorealism? Several answers are possible. First, it is likely that the unflinching realism of the films, showing the desolation of Italy in the late 1940s, met with a positive response from audiences who had lived through the cataclysmic violence and brutality of World War II. Mixed with the unsparing picture of poverty was a message of solidarity and hope—between people of differing religious and political beliefs, between nations, between family members. The combination of realist observation and hope is a very attractive feature of these films.

A second factor accounting for the interest of neorealist films would be their oppositional status in relation to Hollywood films. Nineteen forty-six was the peak audience year for Hollywood films in the United States, and in Western Europe these films swept triumphantly into newly liberated countries. In this atmosphere, neorealist films were important to European intellectuals because they showed that there was a viable, original European film culture independent of Hollywood models. This was particularly important in Italy, where neorealism is still considered the cornerstone of national film culture, though it also played a large role in France, where André Bazin and other critics considered the neorealist filmmakers to be a vital part of a distinctively European film tradition. Neorealism also served as a rallying point for those who felt that Hollywood left out vital areas of human experience such as art, politics, and sexuality. Much of the American critical response to neorealist films stressed their artistic and universal qualities. Political elements could also be gathered from the neorealist films—for example, the popular front sentiments of *Open City* (1945).

The area of sexuality requires more detailed attention. *Open City*, the first foreign-language film to earn more than a million dollars in the United States, certainly is not sexually explicit by contemporary standards. But some observers felt that *Open City's* success in the United States was based on a salacious advertising campaign.[11] Although *Open City* is known today for its themes of resistance and solidarity and its bold realist style, the film does include some sexually frank and unusual material. *Open City* is basically two films: a story of heroism and suffering (the characters in the Resistance) and a story of decadence and cruelty (the German characters and their Italian girlfriends). The latter story was evidently the source of the ad campaign. This aspect of *Open City* features lesbianism, sexual favors exchanged for luxury items and drugs, and torture. Both "stories" of *Open City* can be seen as prefiguring important trends in the art film. The realist-heroic story anticipates a continuing quest for realism and political subject matter outside of Hollywood norms, whereas the decadent/sexual story anticipates the psychosocial linkages of sex and politics that often take the Second World War as their preferred subject matter (see, for example, *The Damned, The Conformist, The Night Porter*).

The success of *Open City, Paisan* (1946), and *Bicycle Thief* (1947) in the American market opened the door for the distribution of European art films in the United States. By the early 1950s theaters in many American cities presented art films on a regular basis. A similar expansion of art-film outlets occurred in Great Britain and Western Europe, and a number of countries began making films with the international art-film market in mind. In the 1950s important filmmakers from around the globe became esteemed contributors to the art-film circuit: Ingmar Bergman from Sweden; Akira Kurosawa from Japan; Satyajit Ray from India; Luis Buñuel from Mexico (Buñuel, a Spaniard, also made films in France during this period). It is worth pointing out that all of these filmmakers were introduced to international distributors, critics, and audiences primarily by means of the Cannes and Venice Film Festivals. The Cannes Festival, which began in 1946 with *Open City* as a prizewinner, quickly became the leading showcase for the international art film.

Art-film distribution in the United States in some cases singled out one director from a national film industry: Bergman from Sweden, Satyajit Ray from India. However, Great Britain, France, and Italy imported fairly large numbers of films to American art theaters. The British, helped by a common language, offered such prestige films as Olivier's Shakespeare adaptations, David Lean's versions of Dickens, and a variety of light comedies to the art-house market. France offered the fantasy of Cocteau, the comedy of Tati, and the realism of Clément and Clouzot. In Italy, the shared style of neorealism was supplanted in the 1950s by the more individualized films of Fellini, De Sica, Visconti, and Antonioni, and by a number of comedies. Not all of these films were specifically made as art-house pictures; in many cases a film which combined prestige with broad audience appeal in Europe could find only limited release in the United States. So, the opening of the American market to foreign films remained relative: foreign-language films could find audiences only in large cities and university towns, and the broad American public continued to prefer American films to foreign product.

What accounted for even this relative openness of American audiences to foreign films after World War II? Michael Mayer gives a long explanation of factors contributing to the greater interest in foreign films. His major points include: an increasingly cosmopolitan and sophisticated American public; a change in sexual mores, leading to frustration with the Production Code governing American film; a decline in the number of American films produced each year, creating increased opportunities for European film; and a shift toward more ambitious and adult movie subjects, caused by television's takeover of routine entertainment.[12] Mayer's explanation is particularly good on economic conditions. He attributes the decline of Hollywood production to the "Paramount" antitrust decree splitting production and distribution of films from film exhibition. This undermined the Hollywood studio system, and opened the American market to films from other suppliers. "Unwittingly," says Mayer, "a great favor was done for foreign films."[13]

Robert Ray describes the new acceptance of foreign art films with a sweeping generalization, positing that after the experience of World War II the American film audience split into two groups: a majority still accepting the optimistic mythology of traditional American genres and a significant minority demanding a more realistic appraisal of individual and social problems. The significant minority would be the audience for foreign art films as well as for new types of American film (e.g., film noir and the "social problem film") which were in some ways critical of American society.[14] Mayer's and Ray's explanations are clearly complementary. Mayer describes some conditions necessary for the increased exhibition of art films in the United States, and Ray provides the underlying reason for positive audience response to these films.

Ray's explanation of the popularity of art films in America would account for their degree of success in Europe as well. Hollywood film had been the most popular, best-loved cinema in the world since the end of World War I. With the multiple shocks of World War II, which affected Europe far more strongly than the United States, it seems reasonable that a substantial portion of the European public would no longer be willing to accept the reconciliatory optimism of American film, and would be searching for alternatives. This explanation might in fact account for the *production* as well as the reception of art films in Western Europe after World War II.

However, the post-neorealist history of the art film involves a reevaluation, not a rejection, of American filmmaking. Instead of objecting to Hollywood cinema, a number of European intellectuals interpreted it "against the grain." That is, complexities of social statement and personal expression were "read into" films while conservative elements of Hollywood style (genres, the star system, the happy ending) were minimized. This happened most noticeably in the work of the *Cahiers du Cinéma* critics in France, who were soon to become internationally known film directors. These critics praised the balance between popular cinema and personal expression in Hollywood film, and critiqued the narrowly literary French cinema of the 1950s. At the same time, the *Cahiers* critics did single out a group of European precursors—Vigo, Renoir, Rossellini, Cocteau, Bresson, Tati—as examples of individualized, artistic filmmaking.

The critics of *Cahiers du Cinéma* (François Truffaut, Jean-Luc Godard, Claude Chabrol, Jacques Rivette, Eric Rohmer, et al.) also articulated a theoretical and practical position on film production. This position held that film was an art of individualized expression, even when made in the "big business" environment of the Hollywood studio system. The director was singled out as the individual creator, or "auteur," and the position was known as the "politique des auteurs." The first full statement of the politique des auteurs was François Truffaut's article "Une Certaine Tendance du cinéma français" in *Cahiers du Cinéma* 31 (1954), and the first example of a consciously "auteurist" film criticism was Truffaut's "Aimer Fritz Lang," in the same issue of *Cahiers*.[15] The "politique des auteurs" was later popularized in the United States by Andrew Sarris under the name "auteur theory."

Although the "politique des auteurs" as presented by *Cahiers du Cinéma* in the mid-1950s was largely a defense of the creativity of Hollywood films, this critical position had an enormous impact on the European art film. The idea that the director was, or should be, the artist, fit low-budget art films far better than large-scale Hollywood epics. With the auteur theory, a case could be made that filmmakers were individual artists equivalent to poets, painters, or novelists. This romantic notion of individual creation affected not only criticism, but also film production. It became the rallying cry of Truffaut, Godard, and other members of the French New Wave, and then for would-be art-film directors around the world. Writer-directors were soon the norm for the art film, thus advancing the cause of personal expression. Star directors became almost as well-known as actors, and their new fame gave directors more leverage in dealing with producers and backers. Despite these changes, the auteur theory's case for individual creation in feature filmmaking seems overstated even in relation to the art film, since it leaves out the influence of collaborators, economic and organizational factors, and social influences. Film is a far more collective art than poetry or painting. The auteur director is at best the leader of a process of film production; he or she does not make the film alone.

Spectatorship at foreign films was part of the stereotype of the American intellectual in the 1950s, along with dark glasses, berets, poetry readings, and jazz. It was very much a minority taste, with approximately 600 American theaters out of 15,000 total showing art films all or part of the time in 1955.[16] However, beginning about 1958 and extending into the mid-1960s, the art film burst out of its minority taste-culture and began to attract a much broader audience. From a production standpoint, this change seems directly related to an extraordinary outpouring of art films from France, Italy, and Great Britain. In France, the New Wave demonstrated that low-budget, artistically ambitious films by young directors could reach a surprisingly large national and inter-

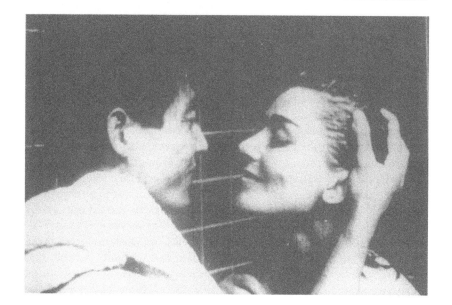

national audience. The New Wave films of Godard, Truffaut, Chabrol, Alain Resnais, and others were new and intriguing in their appeal to an audience of alienated youth, in their breakdown of film conventions, in their exuberance of technique and seriousness of purpose. The 1959 Cannes Film Festival marked a coronation of the New Wave: Truffaut won the Best Director Prize for *The Four Hundred Blows*, Marcel Camus won the Golden Palm (first prize) for *Black Orpheus*, and Resnais' out-of-competition *Hiroshima mon amour* was the most discussed and most widely admired film of the Festival. Meanwhile, in Italy, Fellini and Antonioni were both directing a series of masterpieces, and Rossellini, Visconti, Germi, and others were also receiving international praise. In England, the Angry Young Men films of Tony Richardson, Jack Clayton, Lindsay Anderson, Karel Reisz, and John Schlesinger marked as decisive a break with traditional cinema as the New Wave had in France.

The leading personality in the breakthrough of foreign art films to larger audiences in the United States was not Fellini or Resnais, however, but rather the French actress and sex symbol Brigitte Bardot. Bardot's film *And God Created Woman* (1956), directed by her then-husband Roger Vadim, earned four million dollars in the United States in 1958, an astonishing amount for a foreign film at that time. The film presents Bardot as a kind of female James Dean, a young, rebellious character who distrusts authority and established values and follows her own emotions.[17] Well shot in widescreen and featuring a naturalistic look at the picturesque village of St. Tropez (not yet a world-famous resort), the film had been a popular and critical success in France. Distributed by a small, independent company, Kingsley International, it started as an art film release in the United States but quickly moved to the major theater circuits in both subtitled and dubbed versions. The film's flouting of conventional morality and its glimpses of skin evidently shocked and exhilarated 1958 audiences.

And God Created Woman's impact on the film industry was significant. New Bardot films were eagerly snapped up by distributors, and old Bardot films were released or re-released. Prices for distribution rights to foreign films escalated overall, so that Ingmar Bergman as well as Bardot's producers benefitted. Explicit sexuality became expected in foreign films, to such an extent that "foreign film," "art film," "adult film," and "sex film" were for several years almost synonyms. More interestingly, many of the successful foreign imports of the period were not merely explicit but thoughtful, sophisticated works as well. *The Lovers* (1958), *Room at the Top* (1959), *Hiroshima mon amour* (1959), *Breathless* (1959), *L'Avventura* (1959), *La dolce vita* (1959), and *Two Women* (1960): each was sexually daring for the period, but much more

than a "skin flick." For a few years, so-called adult films were not necessarily exploitative and reductive.

Although there was clearly an audience for the new, sexually explicit art films, these films also faced enormous censorship pressures. A
film such as *And God Created Woman* or *The Lovers* was likely to
encounter censorship problems in the United States, Canada, Great
Britain, Italy, Japan, and Latin America, and to be banned entirely in the
most conservative European countries (e.g., Ireland). In many cases,
contradictory censorship laws or exposure to unpredictable local censorship made the commercial potential of an art film extremely uncertain. Further, the distributors of such films risked social vilification as
well as high legal bills. These factors may explain why the major Hollywood companies stayed away from producing or distributing sexually
provocative films despite their earnings potential. The major companies
were committed to the conventional morality represented by the Motion Picture Production Code, and to protecting their commercial interests by avoiding social controversy. Small American distributors such
as Kingsley International, Lopert Pictures, Burstyn-Mayer, and Embassy
Pictures distributed foreign films and led the fight against movie censorship. The major companies did occasionally, however, invest in their
smaller competitors: Columbia co-financed some of Kingsley International's foreign film purchases (this included an investment in *And God
Created Woman*), and United Artists in 1958 bought out Lopert Pictures.

Another factor vital to the commercial success of the art film in the
United States circa 1960 was a rapid decrease in Hollywood production.
The American film industry, which had produced 350 to 400 feature
films per year between 1944 and 1951, dropped its output to 258 films
in 1958, 181 films in 1959, and 151 films in 1960.[18] The reduced number
of productions resulted from a loss of more than half the American film-
going audience in a very brief period. Weekly movie attendance in the
United States fell from 90 million in 1948 to 40 million in 1958, due
to competition from television plus changes in urban and suburban
lifestyles.[19] Faced by such a frightening erosion of their home market,
the Hollywood film companies naturally cut production drastically. But
these cuts made the American film industry highly vulnerable to foreign competition. Many exhibitors, instead of going out of business due
to a shortage of American product, turned as a last resort to showing art
films (often of the sexually explicit type). Though not always successful,
this strategy did work in many urban areas, thereby creating an opportunity for European films.

The combination of art, sexuality, and economic opportunity led
to an unprecedented penetration of the American box office by European films in the period 1958–1963. Whereas in the previous twelve

years, a box-office take of one million dollars had been very rare for even the most successful art film, in these years it became almost common. Fellini's *La dolce vita*, De Sica's *Two Women*, Jules Dassin's *Never on Sunday* (1959), and Richardson's *Tom Jones* (1963) were among the remarkable box-office successes of this period. *Tom Jones*, with its freeze-frames and iris shots borrowed from Truffaut's *Jules and Jim* (1961), grossed sixteen million dollars in the United States in 1963–1964 and won the Academy Award for Best Picture of 1963. In terms of gross receipts, foreign film rentals in the United States rose from about $16,000,000 in 1957 to $30,000,000 in 1958, $50,000,000 in 1959, and $69,000,000 in 1961, before dropping off to $49,000,000 in 1962. Although these receipts are skewed by different methods of defining what constitutes a foreign film, with American-financed British films as the major problem, nevertheless the rapid upward trend is unmistakable.[20]

Even with the combination of art and sexuality, the period from 1958 to the mid-1960s should not be seen as a golden age when art films ruled America's screens. Despite the example of *Tom Jones*, art films did not in general displace Hollywood entertainment films from the top of the box-office charts. Further, in 1964 American-made films, most of them from major companies, had more screen time in New York art theaters than films from any other nation.[21] So, the American public's greater interest in art films must be kept in proportion. What happened in the late 1950s and early 1960s was not a sharp break in audience expectations but rather an evolution of tastes. The significance of this evolution was, however, magnified by Hollywood's confusion in this period about the nature of its audience (the early 1960s was the era of *Cleopatra*, a highly publicized, enormously expensive flop), and by the feeling among both filmmakers and critics that European filmmakers were in some way "ahead of" their American counterparts.

In response to the heady successes of 1958–1963, the art film expanded in three directions. First the non-English-language art cinema flourished through the 1960s and into the early 1970s. The established masters—Fellini, Resnais, Godard, Bergman—continued to make excellent films, and they were joined by younger talents such as Bellocchio and Bertolucci in Italy. Further, the low-cost, high-prestige approach of art cinema quickly spread around the world, so that about 1970, noted art-film directors included Glauber Rocha of Brazil, Ousmane Sembene of Senegal, Jerzy Skolimowski of Poland, and Dusan Makavejev of Yugoslavia. Also, new film festivals were organized to celebrate and support the flourishing of the art cinema. For example, the London Film Festival (established 1963) and the New York Film Festival (established 1965) became showcases for European art films.

A second path taken by the art film was a move toward American auteurs and American art films. Several of the most interesting American films of the late 1960s were low-budget films of personal expression—e.g., *Bonnie and Clyde* (1967), *The Graduate* (1967), *Easy Rider* (1969), *Midnight Cowboy* (1969). Some of these films were specifically planned as European-style works. *Bonnie and Clyde*, for example, was written with Truffaut and Godard in mind, and was directed by Arthur Penn only when the two French filmmakers were not available. For *Midnight Cowboy* a young British director, John Schlesinger, told a story of Manhattan hustlers with a mixture of realism and decadence modeled on his own film *Darling* (1965) and on such art film precursors as *La dolce vita*.

In the seventies, a new generation of self-consciously auteurist American directors became prominent. These directors included Francis Coppola, George Lucas, and Martin Scorsese. They tended to be more entertainment-oriented and more genre-driven than their European counterparts, but they did try to practice film-as-personal-expression within the Hollywood system. And as Coppola, Lucas, and their generation became more obviously commercial, a group of "independent" directors including John Sayles (*Return of the Secaucus Seven*, 1980), Jim Jarmusch (*Stranger than Paradise*, 1984), Spike Lee (*She's Gotta Have It*, 1986), and Gus Van Sant (*Drugstore Cowboy*, 1989) kept alive the idea of personal feature filmmaking in the United States.

The third direction taken by the art film was a move toward European-American hybrids, combinations of American and European approaches to filmmaking. This pathway is the central subject of my book.

2. Economic Links

Before 1914, the most active film exporting nations were France and Italy, with the United States third. Much of the American export trade was handled by British middlemen operating in London, and this structure limited American efforts to compete in the world market. With the advent of World War I, however, European production and distribution diminished and American exports to non-combat regions (e.g., South America, Asia, Australia, and New Zealand) expanded enormously. At the war's end, the American film industry was established as the world leader, with distribution offices around the globe, and it has never relinquished that position. [1]

In the period between the World Wars, the American film industry was involved in European film industries primarily as a distributor of American films. The main business of the American studios was production, distribution, and exhibition in the United States. European distribution was a profitable sideline, but earnings in the United States were so much greater than those from any other country that export was not a high priority in production planning. American companies were not, at this time, heavily involved in European production, except to minimally fulfill the quota requirements of some European governments. In England, for example, American film companies were required to produce a certain number of British-made films in exchange for import licenses. Some high-quality films were undoubtedly made under this arrangement, but a more typical result was the production of "quota quickies," cheaply made films which were thrown together only to meet the quota. The large American film companies were, as a group, making several hundred feature films per year between 1920 and 1945, so they had little reason to compete with themselves by investing in European films.

The interest of the American majors and independents in Europe changed dramatically after World War II, for several reasons. First, repeating the experience of World War I, the devastation of Europe after World War II offered American companies a striking competitive advantage. The Western European countries, except for Great Britain, had been cut off from American films for several years, so the Hollywood companies suddenly had a backlog of hundreds of films to exploit in new markets. Further, the Western European countries (*including* Great Britain) were heavily dependent on American economic aid, and so had difficulty imposing quotas or other restrictions on American films as they attempted to rebuild their own film industries. American companies therefore had an excellent commercial opportunity in Europe in the immediate post-war period.

Another reason for American emphasis on Europe in the post–World War II period was the 1948 Paramount decree, already mentioned in Chapter 1, which limited the American operations of the major American studios by separating production and distribution from exhibition. This Supreme Court decision made it more difficult for the studios to plan and control all aspects of the American film business and therefore led to a drop in the number of films produced. In the new, uncertain business climate thus created, the export market became increasingly important. And in Europe, American antitrust legislation did not apply; indeed, monopolistic practices were encouraged by the U.S. government. Under the Webb-Pomerene Act of 1914, American industries were allowed to organize on an industry-wide basis to encourage exports. The Motion Picture Export Association, formed under this act as the exporting arm of the Motion Picture Association of America, has been a powerful force in the international film business, often negotiating directly with foreign governments. Also, the largest American companies have been able to join together in worldwide distribution organizations unaffected by antitrust legislation.

European markets became a necessity, not a luxury, to American film companies in the 1950s, because the American audience for motion pictures was rapidly shrinking. The American audience for films declined consistently between 1946 and the early 1960s (a period of temporary stability), due to competition from television and from a plethora of other new, or newly popular, leisure-time pursuits (spectator and participatory sports, do-it-yourself activities, trips by car, and so on). Also, demographic patterns shifted: many families moved to the suburbs, far away from the downtown, first-run theatres, and the post-war baby boom kept young adults close to home. The European market was slower to feel the effects of television, suburbanization, and the new leisure-based society, which means that film viewing remained fairly constant through the 1950s and 1960s. In 1958 there were less than 13,000,000 television sets in Western Europe, and 8,300,000 of those were in Great Britain.[2] Film audiences had begun to decrease in

Britain and France—in France, the decline began before the widespread penetration of television. However, the Italian market for motion pictures remained strong, with about 750,000,000 admissions per year through the early 1960s. Italy, for many years the second-largest market for motion pictures in the Western World (the American market remained the largest), was a favored partner for American motion picture activities in Europe in the years 1950–1975.

European governments responded to the enormous competitive advantage of the American film industry after World War II with a number of measures designed to protect local film industries. Quota systems were re-established, despite the efforts of the Hollywood companies, the Motion Picture Export Association, and the United States Department of State. Subsidy programs to support local production were established. Imported films were heavily taxed; in some cases, these taxes were used to support the subsidy programs. Ceilings were put on the earnings of foreign distribution companies. Beyond a level established by law, all such earnings were blocked, meaning that they could be invested nationally but could not be directly remitted abroad. The exact measures varied from country to country, but both the larger Western European nations (Britain, France, Italy, Spain, West Germany) and the smaller nations (Belgium, the Netherlands, and the Scandinavian countries) enacted legislation to protect local film industries from American competition.

It is important to note that protectionist measures were motivated by both economic and cultural policies. Economically, European governments were trying to support national industries and to keep skilled workers employed. But several European governments, notably France, Italy, and Sweden, were also trying to protect the cinematic expression of national culture. The distinction between economic and cultural support can be seen clearly in an analysis of subsidy programs. There are two basic types of subsidy. The first type supports the commercial side of filmmaking by returning to the producers a "bonus" based on a percentage of a film's gross receipts in the national market, or (more recently) by pre-sale of television rights to a state-controlled TV network. The second type supports quality or artistic films by providing production funds to selected screenplays, or by giving monetary prizes to finished films. France and Italy used (and continue to use) both types of subsidy. The support of cinema by cultural as well as economic subsidies should, in theory, provide a bulwark against American competition by sustaining strong national film cultures.

European film industries also benefited from a number of co-production agreements designed to increase the resources available for film production. A co-production is a collaboration between producing companies from two or more nations, under terms defined by formal agreements between the countries involved. The agreements specify how the financing will be handled, and what percentage of actors and technical crew must come from each of the participating nations. Co-productions benefit from a larger pool of available capital, access to at least two national markets, and, very importantly, subsidies from two (or more) participating nations. Although co-productions had been tried in the 1920s, without formal legislation, they became common practice only after World War II.[3] They are now so well established that many high-quality European films are co-productions between two or three nations, with France and Italy the most frequent partners. In France, the number of co-productions in a given year has at times been greater than the number of strictly national productions.

Co-productions are regarded by most European filmmakers and critics as a necessary and positive aspect of film production. They can, however, impose awkward requirements on the filmmaker, especially in the area of casting. Until the early 1980s, co-productions generally required that at least one important role be played by an actor from the minority co-producing country. Because of this requirement it is typical to see Germans acting in French films, Italians acting in Spanish films, and so on. In many cases such international casting causes no problems. Either the French actor plays a French character in an Italian film, or the actor can function effectively in a foreign context. Dominique Sanda, for example, has given marvelous performances in Italian films (*The Conformist*, 1971; *The Garden of the Finzi Continis*, 1972; *1900*, 1976; *The Inheritance*, 1978). However, the casting in co-productions can also be disconcerting, especially when dubbing is involved. For example, in *Two Women*, an Italian-French co-production, Jean-Paul Belmondo is dubbed by an Italian actor. He loses his distinctive voice, and therefore much of his force as an actor. The hazards of co-production are satirized beautifully by Godard in *Masculine-Feminine* (1966), where the Swedish actors imposed by co-production are presented only in a film-within-a-film where their dialogue consists of grunts. Godard here comments on the problems of co-production by insisting on the arbitrariness and awkwardness of inserting a Swedish element into a French film.

In the 1980s co-production requirements were modified so that director, writer, cast, and crew could come from any European Economic Community (EEC) country. These changes brought European film industries into line with the EEC's "open market" philosophy. However, it is still typical for co-productions to feature international casts with at least one main actor from the minority producing country. The continuance of this system probably has to do with marketing requirements in the participating countries, and with informal under-standings between co-producing partners.

European protective measures and co-production agreements did succeed in creating some room for national cinemas to rebuild and de-velop. They did not eliminate American competition from the European market. In most cases, even quota systems did not prevent American films from taking a large percentage of box-office receipts from Euro-pean markets. Only in France and occasionally in Italy have local films outgrossed American imports in the period 1946–1989, and even in these countries the United States has remained, by a large margin, the leading exporter represented in the national market.

Economic factors certainly account for some of this American dominance. The American film industry benefits from an enormous lo-cal market. This market declined from 4.5 billion spectators in 1946 to approximately 920 million spectators in 1970, but it is still much larger than the market for film admissions in any European country. With such a large local market, American companies can spend more money on producing an individual film, and thus gain a competitive advantage over European producers. Further, the American market has since 1918 been more or less "closed" to foreign imports, not because of protection-ist laws but because of the economic strength of the American film com-panies plus the preference of American audiences for English-language films using established stars and genres. Even the record $69,000,000 earned by imported films in the United States in 1961 was only about 7.5% of the gross box-office receipts of that year.[4] American companies also have access to excellent international distribution networks that are not available to European distributors. Since World War II the American major studios have been the only truly international film distributors, with offices in North America, Europe, South America, Asia, and Africa. This means that a European producer has two options in exporting a film: sell rights on a country-by-country basis, which is time-consuming and risky; or arrange distribution with an American company, if pos-sible, and share earnings with that company.

However, purely economic factors do not entirely explain Ameri-can dominance of the world trade in motion pictures. (Let us note in pass-ing that although the United States is by far the largest exporter of motion pictures, India is the largest producer. India's several hundred films per year are intended primarily for that country's national market.)[5] It must be pointed out that American films are, and have been, widely popular with international audiences. Other important film-producing countries (e.g., France, Italy, Great Britain, the Soviet Union) have not been able to duplicate the American film's broad-based and long-lasting appeal. This appeal has been so great that at times film exhibitors in

Western European countries have allied themselves with the American studios and against their own film production industries so as to enjoy the profits stemming from exhibition of American films.

The protective measures installed by European governments have not always succeeded in controlling the American film industry's presence in Western Europe, but they have—in combination with other factors—led to some important modifications of American film industry practice. The blocked funds, designed to rectify severe balance-of-payments problems, encouraged American companies to make films abroad. If they could not directly remit funds to the United States, they could make films abroad and then distribute these films both in the United States and internationally. This scheme had two additional advantages beyond the utilization of otherwise unavailable revenues. First, production costs in the United States were extremely high because of union rules, talent costs, and studio overhead charges. European production costs—even those which were not covered by blocked funds—were much cheaper. Labor regulations were more flexible, and currency exchange rates were extremely favorable, especially in Italy, Spain, and other Southern European countries. These conditions were so tempting that so-called "runaway production" became a serious problem for American film workers. Unemployment in the Hollywood film community ran very high in the 1950s and 1960s, and congressional hearings were called to examine the threat of overseas production to American workers. Second, the European market was becoming more and more crucial to Hollywood companies. Producing films in Europe, with local as well as American stars, and with publicity directed to European as well as American media, could help to attract a European audience. The 1950s and 1960s were the great years of European stars, especially women, in American-produced films: Sophia Loren, Gina Lollobrigida, Anna Magnani, Brigitte Bardot, Jeanne Moreau.

The European-American film collaborations of the 1950s were not, in general, high-quality syntheses of the best of both industries. Some "A" pictures were made involving top American talent and unique European locations: for example, Hitchcock's *To Catch a Thief* (1954), with Cary Grant and Grace Kelly, filmed on the French Riviera. However, it was more typical to make spectacle films which took full advantage of the low cost of European labor, costumes, and sets: for example, Biblical epics (*The Ten Commandments*, 1956), Greek and Roman subjects (*Ben Hur*, 1959), adventure and war films of the distant past (*The Vikings*, 1958). The spectacle films achieved a lavish scale—especially when blocked funds were involved—that would have been unthinkable in the United States. Peter Besas reports that for United Artists' *Alexander the Great* (1955), shot in Spain with blocked funds, the production team was told that the "sky was the limit." Principal photography on *Alexander* took twelve months, and was followed by two months of additional shooting.[6]

Runaway productions continued into the 1960s, with many of the most spectacular and most prestigious "Hollywood" films of the decade being made abroad. Some examples of high-quality runaway productions are: in 1962, *Lawrence of Arabia*, *The Longest Day*, and *Taras Bulba*; in 1963, *Cleopatra*, *The Great Escape*, *Charade*, *The Fall of the Roman Empire*, and *55 Days at Peking*; in 1964, *Becket*, *Dr. Strangelove*, and *The Train*; in 1965, *A Funny Thing Happened on the Way to the Forum*, *A Man for All Seasons*, and *The Bible*. By this time, blocked funds were no longer a major problem, but there were other good reasons to film in Europe. Labor costs remained low in relation to Los Angeles, and attracting the European public was still important. Additionally, the subsidy and co-production benefits designed to support local film industries were in most cases made available to Hollywood-financed, made-in-Europe films.

The subsidy laws of France, Italy, Great Britain, and other European countries were all designed so that only national films or qualified co-productions would receive subsidies. Typical requirements had to do with the nationality of the production company and of the filmmakers; at least some of the key creative personnel of an Italian film had to be Italian. However, a locally-based subsidiary of a Hollywood company would be considered French, or Italian, or British for purposes of subsidy. This type of interpretation had a great deal to do with the dramatic rise in Hollywood-financed productions in Great Britain in the 1960s. The British Eady Fund subsidy was particularly generous.

Collaborations between American and European companies are not, strictly speaking, co-productions because they are not structured by specific government-to-government agreements. Also, an American-European collaboration does not offer the same kind of reciprocal subsidies available in Europe, since there is no government subsidy of American film productions. However, American companies can still benefit from the double or triple subsidies of European co-productions, either by working through a European subsidiary or by investing in a film produced by European companies. Sometimes American involvement is clearly stated in the credits of a co-production. In other cases American investment is not acknowledged, because only the European partners qualify for subsidies. For example, *Sodom and Gomorrah* (1963) was officially a co-production between Titanus (Italy) and Pathé (France), and was therefore eligible for French and Italian subsidies. However, this same film also involved the participation of three American companies, MGM, Universal, and Embassy, plus the British company J. Arthur Rank.[7]

In the 1960s American companies took advantage of the subsidy and co-production laws and the strong market for films in Europe to greatly expand their production operations. Instead of simply making American films in Europe, they began investing in European productions. The period 1960–1963 saw a dramatic increase in American investment in non-English-language films. The American strategy of this time was summarized by Mike Francovich of Columbia Pictures, who told Vincent Canby: "If the Italians want Italian pictures, we will supply them."[8] American companies made production deals with many of the leading producers in France and Italy: with Jacques Bar, Raoul Lévy, Roger Vadim, and Gaumont in France, with Dino de Laurentiis, Carlo Ponti, Titanus, Lux, and Dear in Italy. Many of these deals involved big-budget costume dramas, but American companies also backed European art films such as Alain Resnais' *Muriel*, in French; Federico Fellini's *8 1/2*, in Italian; and even Michael Cacoyannis' *Electra*, in Greek.[9]

However, the enthusiasm articulated by Francovich for American-financed European-language production was short-lived. Both the French and the Italian film industries were suffering from over-production in the early 1960s. In France, many of the features by young filmmakers hoping to be the next Godard or Truffaut remained unreleased. Art films by established directors (e.g., *Muriel*) were commercial disappointments, as were big-budget spectaculars (e.g., Raoul Lévy's production of *Marco Polo*). In Italy, over-production quickly ended a New Wave–inspired move toward younger directors and caused financial difficulties for large production companies, including the bankruptcy of Goffredo Lombardo's Titanus.

In the ensuing contraction of the French and Italian industries, greater attention was given to the commercial attractiveness of film projects, and specifically to the possibilities of international marketing. American support for non-English-language projects became more selective but did not entirely disappear. For example, Les Artistes Associés, the Paris-based subsidiary of United Artists, made multi-picture deals in the mid-1960s to finance French-language films by François Truffaut, Philippe de Broca, and Claude Lelouch, three of the most commercially successful New Wave filmmakers. Several of the films produced under these deals featured actors well-known to English-speaking audiences (e.g., Alan Bates in *King of Hearts*, 1967; Candice Bergen in *Live for Life*, 1967). American producers in the mid-1960s also began to finance English-language art films made in Europe.

Overall, the 1960s was a boom time for European cinemas, and the boom was largely supported by American investment. In Italy in particular the distinction between the national film industry and Hollywood film became blurred. Italians worked on large-scale American runaway productions (e.g., *Cleopatra*, 1963); Italians made their own large-scale spectaculars with American stars (e.g., *The Bible*, 1965); Italians began making distinctive and successful Spaghetti Westerns (e.g., *For a Fistful of Dollars*, 1964); American stars appeared in Italian films (e.g., Burt Lancaster in *The Leopard*, 1963). In financial terms, a study commissioned by Italian unions showed that in 1968, 90 billion lire was invested in film production. Of this, 24 billion came from American companies, 45 billion from European co-producers, and only 22 billion from Italian sources, public and private.[10] Bear in mind that a portion of the 45 billion invested by co-producers may also have been American capital.

In Great Britain as well, a 1960s boom in movie production was largely financed by American companies. Britain at this time was a world center of pop culture, exporting rock music (the Beatles, the Rolling Stones), fashion, and also movies. Attracted by this explosion of popular culture, by a shared language, and by generous government subsidies, the Hollywood studios opened London production offices. For a brief period of time, these offices sponsored a number of projects which were more experimental, more risk-taking, than the typical Hollywood film of the time. Some prominent examples are *Tom Jones* (1963), *A Hard Day's Night* (1964), and *Blow-Up* (1966).[11] An economic overview of the period shows that the British film industry was essentially taken over by American companies in the 1960s. Thomas Guback reports that, "As investors, American subsidiaries, according to the National Film Finance Corporation, wholly or partially financed more than 60 percent of the British features released on the major theatrical circuits during the decade ending in 1971."[12]

Beginning about 1970, American investment in European production gradually declined, for two basic reasons. First, in a period of financial losses and rapidly changing audience tastes, American companies chose to invest in a new generation of American filmmakers and to phase out more traditional productions (e.g., big-budget musical and adventure films) and unprofitable foreign operations (e.g., the London production offices). The shift to youth-oriented films by young directors was prompted by the unexpected success of *The Graduate*, *Easy Rider*, and other low-budget films of the late 1960s. The "youth movement" in Hollywood films continued into the seventies, as many of the most popular films of the decade were directed by young, often film school–educated filmmakers: *The Godfather* (Francis Coppola, 1972); *American Graffiti* (George Lucas, 1973); *Jaws* (Steven Spielberg, 1975); *Taxi Driver* (Martin Scorsese, 1976). These films displayed a sophisticated film style which had largely been learned from European art-film models. Ironically, however, Coppola, Scorsese, and the other American "movie brats" found themselves competing with the European directors they admired in the international marketplace. American studios supported the new American auteurs and withdrew support from European filmmakers.

The second reason for a decline in American investment had to do with an abrupt shrinkage of the European theatrical market for motion pictures. From 1975 through the late 1980s, motion picture audiences in Western Europe dwindled at an alarming rate. In the largest current market, France, the 122 million annual ticket buyers of 1988 were barely 10% of the American market's 1.1 billion spectators of the same year. With local markets reduced to this level, collaborations with European companies were much less attractive to the American studios than in the 1960s. Even subsidy benefits became less interesting, since a subsidy based on gross revenues will not amount to much in a small market. Some of the "lost" European spectators were undoubtedly watching films on television, and European television channels have indeed become involved in film production. But European television companies do not, in general, have the resources to spend several million dollars on a single film project.

The decline of American investment in European production has been accompanied by an increase in the American presence in European movie houses. American films have improved their share of the gross theatrical receipts in France, Italy, Great Britain, and West Germany since 1980. In both France and Italy, the Hollywood industry's share of gross receipts surpassed the national industry's share in the late 1980s. The economic relationship between American and European film industries has thus returned, in some respects, to the conditions of the immediate post–World War II period. Once again, American film is a dominating imported presence, with no serious competition from European film industries.

However, there are several recent developments which may modify the American dominance in European film markets. First, the Hollywood film industry's revenue from theatrical exhibition in Europe is up substantially in the last few years, even though total admissions to movie theaters has not shown the same upward movement.[13] This paradoxical situation has occurred because of higher ticket prices, a weak dollar, and the tremendous success of a few American blockbusters in Europe. Films such as *Pretty Woman, Look Who's Talking, Dances With Wolves,* and *Terminator 2* have done remarkably well in Europe, in some cases earning more in European distribution than in North America.[14] Second, the proliferation of new media outlets in Western Europe, including commercial broadcast television, pay TV, cable, satellite, and home video, has made European markets more important to Hollywood companies. The increased competition between media outlets has driven up demand for high-quality imported programming. Third, the film production business has become increasingly internationalized. American studios have been bought by foreign companies (e.g., Sony's purchase of Columbia, Matsushita's acquisition of MCA/Universal, Rupert Murdoch's controlling interest in Twentieth Century Fox), and many smaller co-ventures are in progress between American, European, and Japanese companies. Also, several European companies are making medium- to high-budget films of their own in English, without relying on major financing from the American major studios. For example, in 1992 the Italian-backed Pentamerica is producing high-profile films starring Jack Nicholson, Tom Selleck, and Kathleen Turner. Fourth, American companies are showing a renewed interest in European production. For example, Paramount has re-opened a London production office, and Warner Brothers has a contract with British producer David Puttnam for a series of European-made films.[15]

These recent developments suggest that European markets are becoming more significant to the international film industry and stimulating new kinds of production activity, while at the same time Hollywood films are not only maintaining but actually increasing their popularity. The complex interplay of European and American competition and collaboration in motion pictures continues to unfold.

STATISTICS

Table 1 charts the total admissions for Theatrical Motion Pictures in France, Italy, Great Britain, West Germany, and the United States in the period 1946–1988. Throughout the period, the United States has had the largest national market. A strong national market supports exports by allowing a higher per-unit cost of feature films (assuming that nationally produced films will be well received in the national market). However, in the 1960s European markets were relatively strong in relation to a rapidly declining American market for motion pictures. This means that European countries—Italy, in particular—had an opportunity to compete with the United States in the world film industry. To some extent the West Europeans did compete effectively with the United States during this period, increasing their market share in their own countries, exporting more to the United States, and collaborating with American companies on a broad range of ventures. By 1980, however, the moment of opportunity had ended. Most of the European markets had collapsed, with only France remaining relatively stable.

The strength of a national film production industry cannot in all cases be equated with the size of the national market. In West Germany, for example, the large national audience for motion pictures in the 1960s did not translate into a film production industry which thrived in national and international markets. However, West Germany was constrained from enacting film quota systems and other protectionist laws by its military and political dependence on the United States. The West German film industry therefore operated under less favorable conditions than those which existed in Italy and France.

Table 2 shows the relative strengths of Italian and United States films in the Italian market between 1950 and 1988. The 1970 peak of 60.6% of national receipts for Italian films represents only a brief period of success; in the 1980s American imports dominated the Italian market. Note that the percentages given for Italian films from 1960 on may actually be overstated, because many English-language, multinational films are designated as "Italian" in Italy. For example, both *Last Tango in Paris* and *The Last Emperor* were officially considered Italian films.

TABLE I

ADMISSIONS FOR THEATRICAL MOTION PICTURES *(in millions)*, 1950–1988

Date	France	Italy	W. Germany	U.K.	U.S.A.
1950	357	662	——	1396	3120
1955	390	819.4	767	1182	2392
1960	354.6	744.8	609.6	501	2080
1965	285.8	664	320	327	2288
1970	183.1	525	160.1	193	920
1975	180.7	515	128.1	116	1035
1980	173.7	241.9	143.8	96	1024
1985	172.8	123.1	104.2	71	1056
1988	122.4	92.5	108.9	84	1085

SOURCES: Austin, *Immediate Seating*; Biarese, "Les Structures économiques du Cinéma italien," in *Cinéma* 190–191; Bolzoni, "L'esempio italiano," in *Bianco e Nero* 35.9/12; Contaldo and Fanelli, *L'Affare cinema*; Degand, *Le Cinéma . . . cette industrie*; Perilli, "Statistical Survey of the British Film Industry," in Curran and Porter, *British Cinema History*; *Variety*; *International Motion Picture Almanac*.

TABLE 2
PERCENTAGE OF THEATRICAL RECEIPTS
TO NATIONAL VS. USA FILMS IN ITALY,
1950–1988

Date	Italian Films	USA Films
1988–1989	23	55.6
1978–1979	36	43
1970	60.6	27.5
1965	47	41.1
1960	41.2	45.6
1955	34.8	58
1950	24	67.4

SOURCES: Guback, *The International Film Industry;*
Variety; International Motion Picture Almanac.

3. The Euro-American Art Film: Definition

"Euro-American art film" is an invented term, a phrase created to describe a category of film which has previously been only vaguely and uncertainly perceived by historians. Although my definition describes a fairly broad tendency in recent film production, there will be questions about whether specific films and filmmakers fit the definition. Each film has some degree of uniqueness; no film is made to fit *a posteriori* critical definitions. However, the films I label "Euro-American art films" were made, at least to some extent, to fit audience expectations. They were produced, promoted, and distributed as syntheses of European and American film. Therefore, the critic/historian's job here, as with other categories of film (e.g., genres and movements), is not to propose a totally new category of film, but rather to develop an explicit and consistent definition for a category which has previously been vague.

The problem of defining the Euro-American art film is most similar to the problem of defining film noir. In each case the group of films was without a name for a period of time—although American films noirs were made primarily in the 1940s and 1950s, no consistent name was found for them until the early 1970s.[1] A definition of film noir eventually formed around a series of characteristics which were shared to a greater or lesser extent by individual films. My definition of Euro-American art films is similarly structured around a series of characteristics shared to a greater or lesser extent by specific films. The definition of film noir is further complicated by disagreements about the defining characteristics and the films to be included, although in both areas there is a good deal of common ground among film historians. Despite the disagreements, the category film noir has proven useful in film scholarship. Indeed, the divergence of definitions and boundaries can be seen as an index of the fruitfulness of the discussion of film noir. I will be pleased if alternate definitions are proposed for Euro-American art films, for this will indicate the usefulness of the category.

The Euro-American art film attempts a synthesis of the European art film and the American entertainment film, with the goal of reaching a much larger audience than the art film normally commands. The characteristics of this type of film are:

1. The film makes prominent, but not always exclusive, use of the English language.

2. One of the film's key collaborators is a European film director.

3. The film is made in the period 1945–present.

4. The film has a larger budget and better production values than a typical European art film.

5. Cast and crew come from two or more countries. At least some of the actors are native English speakers.

6. The film utilizes specific qualities of the European art film (ambiguity, originality, personal style, emphasis on character over plot, connection to other arts).

7. It also utilizes specific qualities of the American entertainment film (stars, genres, presold subjects, spectacle, action).

8. The film is in some way a meeting of European and American cultures.

This basic profile of the Euro-American art film is not terribly complex. Nevertheless, several problems of definition and boundary must be solved to give an adequate notion of my subject. I will discuss these problems of definition following the order of the eight points listed above.

The question of what language is used in a film seems self-evident, but it is not. Some films use more than one language. *Paisan* is in Italian and English; *The American Friend* is in German and English; *Last Tango in Paris* is in French and English; *Contempt* is in French, English, German, and Italian. These films are all good examples of cross-cultural filmmaking, with the linguistic mix indicating the encounter of American and European cultures. A film which has no dominant language, and in which English has a prominent place, should certainly be considered a Euro-American film. But a film which makes only slight use of English (e.g., Wenders' *Wings of Desire*, where English is used by the Peter Falk character and in some song lyrics) is marginal to my subject.

Films made in two or more language versions constitute a more troubling problem of language. Dubbing is a common practice in European film industries. Some films are entirely post-synchronized. Others are partially post-synchronized, with actors dubbed in languages where they are not native speakers. Some actors do their own dubbing, others do not. Sometimes lip movements correspond to the dubbed speeches, sometimes they do not. Co-productions often exist in two or more linguistic versions. For example, in the French-Hungarian co-production *David, Thomas et les autres* (1985), directed by Laszlo Szabo, a French-language version features the voices of Jean-Louis Trintignant and Jean Rochefort, the two stars, but French dubbing for the many Hungarian actors. The Hungarian version features the voices of the bit players, but Hungarian dubbing for the stars. Both versions of this film make compromises in presenting spoken language, and it is impossible to determine the original or primary language of the film.

The Italian film industry is particularly hard to judge in terms of original language version. Almost everything is dubbed in Italy, because of the wide range of dialects and accents in the country, and because the dubbing of foreign and Italian films has been customary since the beginning of the sound period.[2] This means that when an English-language version of a film is required, it is fairly easy for Italian directors and producers to put one together. *Fellini Satyricon* provides a good example. This film, like most of Fellini's films, was post-synchronized. A carefully dubbed English-language version was put together. A carefully dubbed Italian-language version was also put together. Which is the original version of the film? I see no way to make such a distinction.

In an even stranger development based on the Italian predilection for dubbing, many Italian productions are filmed in English and then dubbed for Italy. According to Geoffrey Nowell-Smith, writing in 1968, "In Italy today any film that is made with American capital or with an American distributor's guarantee must first be shot in English and then dubbed into Italian for the home market."[3] This is a bit overstated, since it does not describe the complexities of dubbed films such as *Fellini Satyricon*. But Nowell-Smith is correct to call attention to an English-language presence in American-financed Italian films, a presence which may be manifested by direct-sound filming in English or by filming without sound with at least some actors miming English-language dialogue. The use of English-speaking actors in starring roles is also extremely common in Italian films. The practice of making the English language an important part of Italian films has something to do with the expectations of American and Italian audiences, since Americans dislike dubbing and Italians accept it. However, this practice has an additional significance. It is strong evidence of the pressure of American capital and American culture on the Italian film industry.

In making the director's nationality a criterion of the Euro-American art film I do not mean to indicate unqualified acceptance of the auteur theory. Films are made by groups of filmmakers working in specific social and institutional settings; they do not emerge from the director's forehead. In later chapters of this book, I will describe the contributions of actors, writers, and especially producers to specific films. However, the director is used as a defining characteristic of Euro-American art films for two reasons. First, in most art films the director's reputation is an important part of the film's "package," of the way it presents itself. *Blow-Up* is an English-language film *by Antonioni;* the director's name is an essential component of this type of film in the discourses of production and reception. Second, the art film is primarily a European phenomenon, at least in terms of production, and the great majority of art-entertainment hybrids rely on the prestige of a *European* art-film director.

The question of who is, and who is not, a "European director" remains a thorny one. In a somewhat arbitrary boundary move, I have excluded British film directors from the category "European." This is done not because of political or geographical reasons, but because of a special relationship between the British and the Hollywood film industries. In the absence of language barriers, the British film industry has become, to a large extent, an adjunct of Hollywood. British directors and actors move freely between local and Hollywood productions; British sound studios host American super-productions; British government subsidies for film production go in some years primarily to American companies. Its close ties to American film production have given the British film industry commercial advantages such as increased employment and access to export markets. In a cultural sense, however, the Hollywood connection has been a disadvantage. The migration of actors and directors has enriched the American cinema while impoverishing British film culture. Meanwhile, films made in British studios sometimes lack even the pretense of Britishness (e.g., the *Star Wars* and *Superman* series). The threat to cultural autonomy is so strong that one British producer has commented, "If the United States spoke Spanish, then we would have a film industry."[4]

In the last decade, the British film industry has succeeded in producing a number of films that are British, rather than Anglo-American, in flavor: *The Ploughman's Lunch* (1984), *Letter to Brezhnev* (1985), and *My Beautiful Laundrette* (1985) are a few examples. The television network Channel 4, which is specifically mandated to support independently and regionally produced films, is one factor in this revival. Overall, though, the British film industry is still more closely tied to Hollywood than any other European film industry. My study leaves this special case to other authors, and concentrates on French and Italian filmmakers (with some attention to West Germany, Sweden, Greece, et al).

The British film industry does, however, play a part in this book as an occasional "halfway point" where European and American filmmaking meet. Several European art film directors have made English-language films in Great Britain, using British crews, studios, and locations to make films for American and world markets. Films such as

Fahrenheit 451, Blow-Up, The Canterbury Tales, and *Death Watch* could be called "Euro-Anglo-American art films," with the British setting providing a convenient context for English-language production.

Immigrants are always to some extent between cultures. So is a European director living and working in the United States an American or a European director? I consider émigrés who are well-established in the Hollywood system of production to be primarily American filmmakers. For example, Milos Forman's *One Flew Over the Cuckoo's Nest* and *Ragtime* are American films. Paul Verhoeven, a Dutch filmmaker, seems entirely assimilated into the Hollywood film industry. His American films *Robocop* and *Total Recall* are well-made, high-budget action films, with plentiful special effects. The case of Roman Polanski is more complex. When Polanski directs high-prestige Hollywood films such as *Rosemary's Baby* or *Chinatown* he is an American filmmaker. But Polanski's *Repulsion, The Tenant,* and *Why?* (made in England, France, and Italy, respectively, and all with international casts) fit my definition of Euro-American art films. Polanski, a Polish-born filmmaker who has made English-language films in several countries, might be called an "international wanderer" rather than an émigré.[5]

In a period of multi-national dealmaking and convenient air travel, Polanski may be a more emblematic figure than Verhoeven. Film industry émigrés of the last thirty years have rarely established long, stable Hollywood careers. More typically, they come to the United States to make one or two films and then quickly depart. Some examples of this pattern are Jacques Demy, *Model Shop;* Agnès Varda, *Lions Love;* and Paolo and Vittorio Taviani, *Good Morning, Babylon.* These films retain an outsider's perspective; they are Euro-American rather than Hollywood films. But even Louis Malle and Wim Wenders, who worked for several years in the United States and declared themselves "American filmmakers," were never thoroughly assimilated into Hollywood production. Malle recently returned to France to make *Au revoir les enfants* and *Milou en mai (May Fools);* Wenders returned to West Germany to make *Wings of Desire.* As for Milos Forman, his two most recent films, *Amadeus* and *Valmont,* have combined American and European elements, and the current changes in Eastern Europe may take Forman back to Czechoslovakia. Emigration in the film industry now seems to be provisional.

The topic of émigré directors could be stretched to include five Americans who have worked primarily in Europe: Jules Dassin, Stanley Kubrick, Richard Lester, Joseph Losey, and Orson Welles. A broad survey of Euro-American collaborations in the post–World War II period would include their works. I have chosen not to discuss these five major figures because they would complicate my cross-cultural focus. Europeans responding to American economic constraints and American culture is a different subject from Americans responding to European economic constraints and European culture. The one film by an American expatriate which I discuss at some length is *Never on Sunday*, directed by Dassin, because it was an early and commercially successful English-language art film, therefore a precedent for later filmmaking.

The qualities of the art film listed in point six of the definition are taken from Chapter 1. The qualities of the American entertainment film listed in point seven do not require so much detail, as I assume the reader is familiar with the Hollywood approach to filmmaking. Let me briefly say, however, that Hollywood cinema is a commercially oriented cinema with highly developed and specific strategies for holding the spectator's attention. Action and spectacle are stressed in high-budget productions that are beyond the financial resources of other national film industries. Linear, cause-effect narratives present protagonists who overcome obstacles to achieve their goals. Dialogue is often subordinated to physical action. A "star system" invites audience identification with actors who sustain consistent "star images" from film to film. A "genre system" quickly orients spectators in familiar fictional environments (plot, setting, theme). Hollywood film has also developed and sustained an image of the United States as a land of freedom and economic plenty. These several strategies have proven surprisingly adaptable to cross-cultural contexts. For example, the Western genre's conflict between individual freedom and social responsibility, set in the frontier situation of the American West, has been not only popular but also widely imitated in Western Europe.

Euro-American art films tend to use not only the general strategies of Hollywood cinema, but also specific attributes of those strategies which an international public will recognize as "American." *Contempt* does not simply utilize an American star as its villain. It places Jack Palance, the archetypal Western villain of *Shane* (1953), in the role of the crude and aggressive film producer Jeremy Prokosch.

A Euro-American art film must be a synthesis of the art film and the Hollywood film. A director's reputation is not enough to establish artistic credentials. For example, Vittorio de Sica made some classic art films in the late 1940s and early 1950s: *Shoeshine, Bicycle Thief, Umberto D*. However, most of De Sica's English-language films of the 1960s were frankly commercial ventures. For example, *After the Fox*, starring Peter Sellers, was an imitation of the Pink Panther series of films, and *A Place for Lovers* was an international version of the American hit *Love Story*. Of De Sica's films of the 1960s, I would describe only *The*

Condemned of Altona and possibly *Woman Times Seven* as having art-film qualities. The former, based on a play by Jean-Paul Sartre, describes gradations of guilt, complicity, and moral courage in the rebuilt Germany of 1961. De Sica and scriptwriters Abby Mann and Cesare Zavattini do an interesting job of translating a claustrophobic play into a more naturalistic screen treatment. The latter film shows a cross-section of Italian society via seven vignettes starring Shirley MacLaine. Unfortunately, MacLaine lacks the "reach" as an actress to convincingly portray Italian women of widely varying social backgrounds. Therefore, the film is a botched experiment rather than a post-neorealist tour-de-force.

As the De Sica example suggests, not all English-language European films are Euro-American art films. There are dozens of "international" or "mid-Atlantic" films which do not have artistic pretensions. Some of the English-language European films I have excluded from my history of Euro-American art films are *Smog* by Franco Rossi, *Suspiria* by Dario Argento, *And Hope to Die* by René Clément, *The Inheritance* by Mauro Bolognini, and *The Outside Man* by Jacques Deray. They are not excluded for reasons of quality (*And Hope to Die* and *The Outside Man* are well-made crime films), but rather because they lack the originality and ambiguity of the art film. This kind of judgement is, of course, extremely difficult to make, especially for films at the margin. Whereas *Blow-Up* and *Last Tango in Paris* are clearly art-entertainment hybrids, *Woman Times Seven* is a marginal case.

According to my definition, films could also be excluded for lacking any connection to the American entertainment film. One example of a Euro-American film which departs drastically from Hollywood conventions is Louis Malle's *My Dinner with André*, a two-character, one-location film. This is an "anti-Hollywood" film in its focus on one conversation and exclusion of all else. However, *My Dinner with André* does have characters and a story (albeit attenuated), and it derives much of its interest from creating expectations of a conventional narrative and then not following through. Further, Malle's film was shown in the same theatres as Hollywood films, and attracted a surprisingly large audience. It is not, therefore, a film whose production and reception place it entirely apart from American entertainment film norms. The films of an experimentalist such as Stan Brakhage come much closer to the concept of a non-entertainment film.

THE QUESTION OF GENRE

Euro-American art films do not constitute a genre. They cannot be described as a "popular cinematic story formula," to use Thomas

Schatz's definition of genre.[6] Instead, Euro-American art films should be seen as working between two metageneric categories of film study, the Hollywood entertainment film and the European art film. I call these categories "metageneric" because they are much larger than a single genre; they include genres, but are not bounded by an individual genre. The metageneric quality of the Hollywood film can be accepted as a given. The art film, however, is sometimes called a genre.[7] I would argue that the art film cannot be limited to a single genre, that it includes such "popular cinematic story formulas" as the contemporary drama, the period drama, the love story, the literary adaptation, and the social protest film. David Bordwell's description of the art film as a "mode of film practice" and an alternative to Hollywood filmmaking is an adequate metageneric description of the art film.[8]

If genres are seen much more broadly as "specific networks of formulas which deliver a certified product to a waiting customer" (Dudley Andrew),[9] then Euro-American art films may constitute a genre. They do depend on spectators' experiences of Hollywood films, art films, and art-entertainment syntheses. However, Andrew's definition is so open-ended that it loses the specificity of Schatz's more traditional definition. If genre equals all structurings of audience expectations by means of "networks of formulas," then it becomes a nebulous term. I prefer to locate genres as "story formulas," and to describe Euro-American art films as metageneric.

It might be possible at some point to describe specific narrative/ thematic/stylistic qualities of the Euro-American art film, and how these qualities have changed over time. Such an analysis would make a genre claim for Euro-American art films more plausible. However, in my research on Euro-American art films, I have been struck by the diversity rather than the homogeneity of the films. All Euro-American art films are defined by a "working-between" the American entertainment film and the European art film. But this "working-between" can be quite different from one film to the next. It can be conceptualized as a complex "space" of possibilities and limitations, with both possibilities and limitations changing according to historical circumstances. *Blow-Up, The Canterbury Tales, Contempt, The Last Emperor,* and *Paris, Texas* are very different in their "working-between." The chapters which follow detail how the European art film and the American entertainment film have come together to form a wide range of hybrids.

4. The Euro-American Art Film: History

The previous chapter gives a synchronic, atemporal view of the Euro-American art film. This approach has the advantages of simplicity and clarity; it presents a list of qualities which can then be matched with individual films. The synchronic definition, however, ignores historical process and historical difference. A Euro-American art film of 1955 would have been made in very different conditions from a Euro-American art film of 1985. To understand a history of the Euro-American art film, we must understand the conditions or shaping influences of 1955 and those of 1985, as well as the processes of historical change operating between 1955 and 1985. Therefore, the synchronic definition must be supplemented by a diachronic view so that the Euro-American art film can be analyzed as a phenomenon which develops over time.

The diachronic view cannot, however, be limited to the Euro-American art film as a subject complete in itself. Instead, the one hundred or so films to be studied, stretching over a forty-five-year period, must be embedded in a variety of contexts: political history, economic history, cultural history, and the film histories of the United States and Western Europe. Some of these contexts have already been sketched out in previous chapters. For example, a good deal of the economic background to Euro-American art films can be found in Chapter 2. However, some economic information directly impacting on specific Euro-American films will be included here. Historical material fleshing out the other contexts will also be included as needed.

Film history usually does not divide neatly into decades or other periods. The immediate social context is only one factor shaping a film. The past histories of the creative personnel (director, writer, producer, star), the subject, and the cultural environment will modify any simplistic notion of a film as the direct reflection of current social reality. Also, it is often difficult to accurately date a film to begin with. Scripting, production, European release, and American release may take place over a period of several years. *Blow-Up* was released in the United States in 1966, in Europe in 1967. *The Champagne Murders* was released in Europe in 1967, in the United States in 1968. *Alice in the Cities* was released in Europe in 1973, in the United States in 1977. Where should one place these films in a history of the *interaction* of European and American movies? I have chosen the earlier release date, but there is no perfect way of dating films.

Despite these problems, a rough periodization scheme can be a useful way to show how films respond and contribute to social, economic, and cultural change. Films can be linked to social and ideological currents. Italian neorealism is a useful category for describing a specific cinematic response to social, ideological, and film industry conditions in Italy in the late 1940s. Other periods of film history (and social history) are less clearly marked. For example, when do the contestatory sixties begin in film history? There is no consensus answer to the question. But many Euro-American films of the late 1960s and early 1970s do share a number of contestatory attitudes and characteristics. Some form of periodization is necessary if film history is to be more than a succession of individual films.

Before and during World War II, English-language productions by European (non-British) filmmakers were relatively rare. It is true that a great many émigrés—some famous, some unknown—came to Hollywood to make movies. But directors who remained in France, Germany, or Italy made films in the national languages of those countries. The one brief period of variation from this standard of national films in national languages was 1930–1931, when filming the same script in two or more languages became fairly common as a reaction to the transition from silent to sound movies. Whereas silent movies could be re-titled for different languages, sound films seemed to require shooting the film in more than one language. American companies therefore began shooting multiple-language versions of some of their films; Paramount built a huge studio in France for precisely this purpose.[1] However, multiple-language filming soon proved to be impractically expensive, and was replaced by dubbing. *The Blue Angel* (1930), shot in Germany in German and English versions, is the most famous dual-language film of 1930–1931.

In the period 1946–1958, a few films by Italian or French directors were filmed wholly or partially in English, for widely different reasons. In Italy, as Peter Bondanella has noted, "the encounter of Italy and America in [World War II] and its aftermath" became a favored theme of neorealism.[2] Several neorealist films, including Rossellini's *Paisan* and De Sica's *Shoeshine*, presented the interaction between American soldiers and Italians as part of the texture of everyday life. *Paisan*, whose

PAISAN
The neorealist theme of GIs and Italians.

subject is the communication and miscommunication between Italians and Americans, features several American actors and has a good deal of English-language dialogue. *Paisan* could also be seen as an early, but bizarre, collaboration between a European director and an American producer. It was partially financed by Rod Geiger, who has been described by Federico Fellini (a scriptwriter for Rossellini on *Open City* and *Paisan*) as a drunken sergeant in the U.S. Army who one day wandered into the location where *Open City* was being filmed and offered to sell the film in the United States.[3] Geiger did sell the American rights to *Open City*, and he put up a portion of the money for *Paisan*. He also hired some of the American (non-professional) actors who appear in the film. Geiger thus could be called an American producer of a Euro-American film. But Geiger had no pre-existing ties to the film industry, and he remained a peripherally involved, amateur producer. Geiger's casual and fortuitous involvement with *Paisan* is quite different from the production arrangements made for later Euro-American art films.

A few years after *Paisan*, Rossellini began a series of feature films starring Ingrid Bergman: *Stromboli* (1949), *Europa 51* (1952), *Voyage to Italy* (1953).[4] These films exist in post-synchronized English-language and Italian-language versions. The films combined the talents of a major Hollywood star and a European art-film director. *Stromboli*, the first Bergman-Rossellini film, was financed by RKO based on Bergman's star name. The succeeding films were financed by European producers.

The Rossellini-Bergman films are highly original character studies, rejecting the genre formulas and conventional morality of Hollywood production to explore what Peter Brunette terms "the complexity, the mass of grays, that mark all human relationships."[5] In *Stromboli*, *Europa 51*, and *Voyage to Italy* Rossellini makes extensive use of contrasts between character and landscape to bring out the feelings of the Bergman character in a manner which anticipates Antonioni. These are subtle films which disappointed American critics and audiences in the 1950s, but have since become part of the canon of film history.

A widely reported story says that Vittorio De Sica was offered lavish financial backing for *Bicycle Thief* (1947) by an American producer if he would cast Cary Grant as the unemployed worker. The offer was turned down; the use of a world-famous American star would have destroyed the authenticity of De Sica's neorealist masterpiece. In 1954, however, De Sica did make a neorealist story with American stars for David O. Selznick, the producer who had offered to finance *Bicycle Thief*. This film, which stars Jennifer Jones and Montgomery Clift, is called *Stazione termini* in Italian and *Indiscretion of an American Wife* in English. The dual titles are appropriate, since *Stazione termini—*

Indiscretion is really two films in one. As a neorealist work (with script by Cesare Zavattini), the film can be seen as an exploration of the happenings and characters and environments of a Roman train station. On the other hand, the film is a melodramatic love story involving Jones and Clift, and the love story is not well integrated with the neorealist observations. To heighten the conflicts of meaning, the film includes a highly sentimental score by Alessandro Cicognini which thoroughly contradicts the visuals. *Stazione termini—Indiscretion* is a confused film, an example of how not to put together an American-European collaboration.

In the 1950s the French director Jean Renoir made a group of films which critic Raymond Durgnat has aptly termed "international"[6]: *The River* (1951), *The Golden Coach* (1954), and *Paris Does Strange Things* (1957; French title *Elena et les hommes*). *The River* was an English-language film, made in India; the other films were made in English versions, and French versions, and in the case of *The Golden Coach*, an Italian version. Renoir, in exile from Vichy France, had made films in Hollywood during World War II; this undoubtedly helped him put together productions with an English-language component. The international qualities of these films allowed for different subject matter (*The River*) and more lavish budgets than would have been available for a purely French film. The international aspects of these films also give them a kind of distance from their subject matter. For example, *The Golden Coach* has been widely interpreted as a film about the theater, and not about a particular theater. This effect of philosophical distance is very different from the socially and politically rooted films which Renoir made in France in the 1930s.

In addition to these works by three of the world's great filmmakers, a few other European films of the 1950s mixed English-language filming with aspirations toward art. Renato Castellani directed a version of *Romeo and Juliet* (1954), with British actors in the primary roles and exteriors filmed in Italian locations. This prestige film was produced by the British producer-distributor-exhibitor J. Arthur Rank. Spanish émigré Luis Buñuel filmed *The Adventures of Robinson Crusoe* (1954) for Mexican producer Oscar Dancigers. Additionally, a number of Italian art films used American actors in prominent roles. For example, in Fellini's *La strada*, Fellini's wife Giulietta Masina is joined in the cast by Anthony Quinn and Richard Basehart. Even though *La strada* was released (first-run) and reviewed as an Italian-language art film in the United States, both Italian-language and English-language dubbed versions of the film were made. The Italian-language version features Giulietta Masina's voice and has an Italian actor dubbing Anthony Quinn;

in the English-language version we hear Quinn's voice while Masina is dubbed by an English-speaking actress.

The main pattern we can derive from the films discussed above is that filming in English was slowly becoming an option for European filmmakers in the 1950s. Films with an English-language soundtrack would have had enhanced commercial viability at this time, since the Hollywood studios were producing fewer films and American exhibitors were therefore more open to showing films from other sources. But the large Hollywood companies were not yet supporting English-language films by art-film directors; RKO's financing of *Stromboli* and Selznick's production of *Stazione termini—Indiscretion* are exceptions to this rule.

In 1959 Jules Dassin's *Never on Sunday* was filmed on a low budget in Greece with majority financing from United Artists.[7] Dassin's film, which in pre-production was called "The Happy Whore," tells how Ilya (Melina Mercouri), a good-hearted prostitute, "educates" Homer (played by Dassin himself), an American intellectual visiting Greece. The education consists of directing Homer's attention away from an idealization of the art and drama of ancient Greece, and toward the materiality and sensuality of everyday life. This film earned Mercouri a Best Actress prize at Cannes and an Academy Award nomination. It had a strong commercial career in the United States in 1960, despite a cast of then-unknowns, and despite Dassin's having been blacklisted by the Hollywood studios ten years earlier for his political beliefs.

The success of *Never on Sunday* was precedent-setting in three respects. First, it showed that American investment in English-language, foreign-made art films could be profitable and prestigious. United Artists risked relatively little on the film, and earned both a healthy profit and critical prestige. Second, it was among the first Euro-American films to use the meeting of cultures as a central theme as well as a production situation. This theme has since been used by a number of excellent films. Third, the film paved the way for additional English-language co-ventures between American companies and Greek filmmakers—e.g., *Zorba the Greek* and *The Trojan Women*.

Godard's *Breathless* and Fellini's *La dolce vita*, both released in 1959–1960, are generally considered seminal films of French and Italian cinema, respectively. Without challenging that judgement, I should like to note that both films contain important cross-cultural, European-American elements. In *Breathless*, a cast of unknowns is buttressed by the participation of Jean Seberg, a young American actress who had starred in *Saint Joan* for producer-director Otto Preminger in 1957. Seberg's leading role opposite Jean-Paul Belmondo (who became a star thanks to *Breathless*) allows Godard to explore the theme of cross-cul-

NEVER ON SUNDAY
Melina Mercouri (second from left), Jules Dassin.

Courtesy of the Academy of Motion Picture Arts and Sciences.

LA DOLCE VITA
Anouk Aimée, Marcello Mastroianni.

tural tension and misunderstanding. This theme echoes the Rossellini-Bergman films, and anticipates *Contempt.* As for *La dolce vita*, it is partly set in the milieu of international film production of the "Hollywood sul Tevere" period. The Hollywood-influenced film community of Rome becomes one of Fellini's metonyms for a confused modern amorality. As with *Breathless*, English-speaking actors are prominently featured in *La dolce vita*, with the best-known being Swedish actress Anita Ekberg.

The successes of *Never on Sunday, Breathless*, and *La dolce vita* in 1960 did not immediately start a wave of European-made art films featuring English-speaking actors. It was a few years later, after commercial setbacks to the French New Wave and to the new Italian cinema, that American companies began supporting English-language art films and reducing their investments in French- and Italian-language films. The first American producer to make this switch was probably Joe Levine, an opportunistic producer-distributor who had built his Embassy films into a large company primarily through investments in European films. Levine began his rise by heavily promoting such Italian costume dramas as *Attila* (1958) and *Hercules* (1959). He was also supporting European art films in the early 1960s, often in partnership with the Italian producer Carlo Ponti. In the Ponti-Levine collaborations, Ponti supervised the production and Levine supplied most of the budget. Among the Ponti-Levine collaborations of the 1960s were *Two Women* (1961), *Bocaccio 70* (1962), *Landru* (1963), *Marriage Italian Style* (1964), and *Yesterday, Today, and Tomorrow* (1964). *Landru* was a French-language film, directed by Claude Chabrol and co-produced by Georges de Beauregard; the other films are in Italian. By 1963, Levine had moved into Euro-American, English-language art films, financing such cosmopolitan ventures as *Contempt* (directed by Jean-Luc Godard, starring Brigitte Bardot, Michel Piccoli, Jack Palance, and Fritz Lang) and *The Empty Canvas* (directed by Damiano Damiani, starring Bette Davis, Horst Buchholtz, and Catherine Spaak). Both films were based on novels by the Italian writer Alberto Moravia, and both were shot in Italy. A slightly later Levine film, *The Tenth Victim* (1965), featured Italian star Marcello Mastroianni and the Swedish actress Ursula Andress (known primarily for her English-language movies), with Elio Petri as director. This film was made in Italian-dubbed and English-dubbed versions, and it includes a sequence filmed in New York.

The major Hollywood companies quickly followed Joe Levine's lead, investing in English-language films by well-known European directors. Twentieth Century Fox supported *The Condemned of Altona* (1963), produced by Ponti and directed by De Sica. Fox also produced

Zorba the Greek (1964), starring Anthony Quinn and directed by Michael Cacoyannis, which had a remarkable commercial career in the United States. Levine and Fox combined to back *Woman Times Seven* (1967), directed by De Sica and starring Shirley MacLaine. Universal financed *The Champagne Murders* (1967), directed by Claude Chabrol, a suspense film notable mainly for its production approach; both English-language and French-language live-sound versions were filmed. MGM produced *Viva Maria* (1965), a Western (or perhaps parody Western) filmed in Mexico by Louis Malle and starring Brigitte Bardot and Jeanne Moreau. MGM also supported the Ponti-produced *More than a Miracle* (1967), directed by Francesco Rosi and starring Sophia Loren and Omar Sharif.

An especially interesting film of the period was *The Leopard* (1963), starring Burt Lancaster and directed by Luchino Visconti. Twentieth Century Fox invested in this film when the Italian production company, Titanus, experienced financial problems. The American studio required an American star (Lancaster) and requested English-language filming. In practice, Lancaster spoke English in the film and the other actors spoke Italian. Italian-language and English-language versions were then prepared; the English-language version was much shorter. Although Fox paid for an elaborate English-language dub, supervised by then-unknown Sydney Pollack (later a prominent Hollywood director), critics agreed that the English-language version, 160 minutes long, was inferior. The Italian-language version, 185 minutes long, was released to glowing reviews in the United States in 1983.[8]

In the mid-1960s, American companies also invested heavily in the British film industry. Most of this investment went to films directed by British filmmakers or American expatriates. But as a side effect of American investment, some noted European art-film directors were invited to make films in Great Britain. François Truffaut's *Fahrenheit 451* (1965), starring Oskar Werner and Julie Christie, was financed by Universal. Michelangelo Antonioni's *Blow-Up*, with a British cast headed by David Hemmings and Vanessa Redgrave, was produced by Carlo Ponti for MGM. Roman Polanski, a Polish expatriate, made two films in Britain, *Repulsion* (1965) and *Cul de Sac* (1966), both produced independently by Polanski's fellow Pole Gene Gutowski. The international quality of these two films is enhanced by starring roles for two French actresses, the sisters Catherine Deneuve (*Repulsion*) and Françoise Dorléac (*Cul de Sac*).

The Euro-American art films of 1963–1967 are tremendously varied attempts to reconcile Europe and America, art and entertainment. *Contempt* can be seen as one of several great films based on a misunderstanding between director and producer (Von Stroheim's *Greed* is the classic example). Producers Levine and Ponti were looking for a sexy film to exploit internationally; they received from Godard a brilliant meditation on film, art, and modern angst. The Ponti-Levine-produced *The Tenth Victim*, with its science-fiction story serving mainly as a premise for sadomasochism and sexual display, gives an intimation of what *Contempt* might have been like as an exploitation film. *Zorba the Greek* is a powerful film which works as art and entertainment. Adapted from an excellent novel by Kazantzakis, the film benefits from a fine international cast and from location shooting in Crete. *Viva Maria* successfully transplants two French stars to an entertainment-oriented, more or less Western genre context. *Blow-Up* is a marvelous film which extends Antonioni's vision of modern anomie to the milieu of "swinging London," and which adds an exploration of the interplay between art and reality. *Repulsion* established Roman Polanski as a talented English-language director. *Repulsion's* precise and well-motivated psychological horror story showcases Polanski's ability to control a tight narrative. *The Leopard* is a lavish historical film about the passing of the aristocratic order in nineteenth-century Sicily. Thoroughly Italian in theme, it is stylistically akin to spectacular American costume dramas (e.g., *Gone with the Wind*). *More than a Miracle*, a conventional and impersonal Hollywood version of a fairy tale, is a disappointing film by Italian director Francesco Rosi, usually an acute observer of social and political conflicts. *Fahrenheit 451* is visually beautiful but emotionally uneven. The experience of directing a film in English, a language which he never spoke well, was so frustrating for Truffaut that he never repeated it.

Some of the films in this group are quite close to Hollywood models (*The Condemned of Altona, Viva Maria, The Champagne Murders, More than a Miracle, Fahrenheit 451*); others are highly original (*Contempt, Blow-Up, Repulsion*). Perhaps the only theme uniting many of the films lies in the presentation of sexuality. As with the art films of the 1950s, European-made films in the 1960s broadened the areas of sexuality which could be presented on screen. According to Turan and Zito, European films of the 1960s expanded the boundaries of what could be shown on screen and pushed American films toward more explicit sexuality.[9] Turan and Zito discuss a heterogeneous group of 1960s European films, ranging from the almost clinical *I, a Woman* to the self-consciously artistic *Blow-Up* and *Persona*. Several of the Euro-American films of 1963–1967 participated in this breaking of taboos and exploration of sexuality: *Contempt* with Brigitte Bardot nude from a rear view, *Viva Maria* with a supposedly impromptu striptease by the Bardot and

Moreau characters, *The Tenth Victim* with the sadomasochistic game, *Repulsion* with sexual repression leading to violence. As with the art films of the 1950s, one should not underestimate the importance of sexual display to contemporary viewers of the films. For example, American reviewers of *Contempt* seem fixated on Brigitte Bardot's buttocks to the exclusion of other aspects of the film.

The Euro-American films of 1963–1967 are relatively calm explorations of art-entertainment hybrids within a fairly stable film industry and social situation. In the next period, 1968–1973, this changes dramatically. Many films of this period are socially, sexually, and artistically confrontational. A number of films of 1968–1973 have the ideological slant of the New Left. They favor youth culture, free sexuality, and revolutionary social and political change while opposing capitalism, militarism, and bourgeois morality.

Two films made in Los Angeles in 1969, *Lions Love* and *Model Shop*, provide an intriguing portrait of artistic and youth culture circles at that time. *Lions Love*, directed by Agnès Varda, features Viva, Jerome Ragni, and James Rado along with film director Shirley Clarke. Viva, Ragni, and Rado loll around in the nude for most of the film, but their indolence does not lessen the anxiety caused by TV coverage of Robert Kennedy's assassination (which plays incessantly during the film's action), or the Clarke character's suicidal depression. *Model Shop*, a film directed by Jacques Demy, is about a young man waiting rather aimlessly to be drafted for the Vietnam War. In its visual specificity and muted emotions, *Model Shop* is something like an early 1960s Antonioni film transplanted to the streets of Los Angeles.

One Plus One (1968), directed by Jean-Luc Godard, is one of the earliest and also one of the most self-critical youth culture films. Godard's film, shot in England, juxtaposes a lengthy Rolling Stones recording session with images of black revolutionaries speaking in a junkyard, Eve Democracy (played by Anne Wiazemsky) giving an interview, and a man reading *Mein Kampf* in a bookstore which specializes in pornographic magazines. The film can be interpreted in at least two ways. First, the musicians' steady progress toward a completed song could be seen as an expression of hope. Second, the dissociation between the recording session and the more explicitly political sequences could suggest a confusion and dislocation in the "youth culture" of the time. The second interpretation seems more fitting to me. The Stones, recording "Sympathy for the Devil" in a modern, antiseptic studio, have no connection with the ideologies and events of the real world. They are not cultural revolutionaries, they are entertainers.

The film's producers eventually lessened the fragmentation of

MODEL SHOP
Gary Lockwood, Anouk Aimée.

LAST TANGO IN PARIS
Marlon Brando, Maria Schneider.

Godard's cut of this film by re-editing the ending to include a completed version of the song. The producers also retitled the film, calling it *Sympathy for the Devil*. In Godard's cut—*One Plus One* is his title—the song is deliberately left incomplete.

Zabriskie Point (1970), Antonioni's film of American student revolutionaries, begins with a student takeover of a campus building and ends with a fantasy of a modernist luxury resort (a metaphor for consumer culture) blowing up. This film is hurt by didacticism and by wooden performances from the two leads, Mark Frechette and Daria Halprin. Though beautiful in parts, it is a less convincing view of the American student than Demy's Antonioniesque *Model Shop*.

The most extraordinary group of Euro-American films made during the period 1968–1973 was linked to the Italian producer Alberto Grimaldi. Grimaldi, a lawyer by training, had entered the world of international filmmaking as the producer, in partnership with United Artists, of two of Sergio Leone's phenomenally successful Westerns. In 1967 he expanded from his base of Spaghetti Westerns by signing a contract with United Artists to make prestigious international films with European art film directors. Many, though not all, of the films, were to be shot in English. Grimaldi's announced aim in producing this type of film was to bring the great talents of the art film to a more commercially-oriented cinema, and thus "to bridge screen art and spectacle."[10] The list of films made under the Grimaldi–United Artists contract includes several major works of post–World War II cinema: *Fellini Satyricon* (1969), *Burn* (1970), *Last Tango in Paris* (1972), and the Pasolini "Trilogy of Life" (*The Decameron* [1972], *The Canterbury Tales* [1973], *The Arabian Nights* [1974]).

All of these Grimaldi-produced films are in some way responding to the rapid social change of the 1960s. *Fellini Satyricon* makes clear analogies between the decadence of ancient Rome and the new freedoms of the "hippie" period. Despite its vivid evocations of the joys and terrors encountered by its young protagonists, the film ultimately seems critical of anarchic freedom and quite conservative in its outlook. *Burn*, directed by Gillo Pontecorvo, stars Marlon Brando as a British emissary trying to quell a black uprising on the (fictional) Caribbean island of Quemada. In this most political of the Grimaldi films, the black cause is presented as just, the overthrow of oppression as inevitable. *Burn* can be seen as a threat to American ideology, since it presents revolution in the Western Hemisphere (Castro and Guevara may be relevant analogies here), with an American star cast as the leading counterrevolutionary. The Pasolini trilogy uses three late-Medieval literary classics to imagine a world uninfluenced by industrialism, consumerism, or bourgeois morality. Of the three films, only *The Canterbury Tales* can be considered an English-language work; Pasolini himself favored the English-dubbed rather than the Italian-dubbed version of the film.

Last Tango in Paris, directed by Bernardo Bertolucci, is the best-known of the Grimaldi-produced films. Like *Satyricon* and the Pasolini trilogy, it is daringly and diversely sexual, and therefore a breaker of taboos. *Last Tango* features Marlon Brando as an American expatriate whose wife has recently killed herself, and Maria Schneider as a young Parisienne who is engaged to be married. They meet several times in an empty apartment for sex, sex as a kind of exorcism. Though the film ends tragically, with Schneider shooting Brando, it was widely admired for its psychosocial insights about sexuality. The Euro-American, between-cultures setting of the film contributes to putting the characters in a position where they can meet, and make love, with some degree of liberty from social norms and networks. Because of cultural and other differences (age, experience), preconceptions are minimized. The film does rely on Brando's star image as developed in earlier films, but even here there is a degree of liberty, a new departure allowed by the Brando character's expatriate status and by the intensity and flamboyance of *Last Tango*'s visual and aural style. The swooping camera movements, the photographic emphasis on gold and red, the Francis Bacon paintings of the credit sequence, and Gato Barbieri's jazz score all suggest that this is *not* a Hollywood movie.

Last Tango, an X-rated film, grossed almost $40,000,000 in the United States alone. It was presented in first-run theaters as well as art houses; in today's moral climate many theater chains avoid X-rated products. *Last Tango* was probably the last European art film to strongly impact American audiences with its breaking of sexual taboos; by the time it came out Hollywood films were every bit as explicit as films from Europe, and hard-core pornographic films (most of them made in the United States) were widely available. So, for the last two decades, a sexual dynamic has not been pushing European films onto American screens, even though some American viewers may prefer the more philosophical handling of sexuality in certain European films to the simpler views of sex in mainstream Hollywood movies.

Among the other Euro-American art films of 1968–1973, *Sacco and Vanzetti* (1971), directed by Giuliano Montaldo, uses the famous trial of two Italian-American anarchists in the 1920s to bring up questions of political morality relevant to contemporary events. *More* (1969), the first film directed by Barbet Schroeder, is about Stefan, a young German who leaves home after college and goes to Ibiza with a lovely blonde American (Mimsy Farmer). Despite an unhappy ending, the film gives a romanticized view of young "drop-outs" and drug addiction. Dusan Makavejev's *WR: Mysteries of the Organism* (1971), is a collage film which combines documentary footage on the psychiatrist Wilhelm Reich with vignettes of sexual openness in the United States and a fictional story of sex and repression in Yugoslavia. Makavejev's thesis seems to be that sexual freedom is a crucial component of political freedom.

The Euro-American films of 1968–1973 were not the only English-language films to challenge established social norms and artistic conventions. These years were marked by a number of socially critical and artistically innovative works by American directors: *Easy Rider* (Dennis Hopper, 1969), *MASH* (Robert Altman, 1970), *Carnal Knowledge* (Mike Nichols, 1970), *Five Easy Pieces* (Bob Rafelson, 1970), *Klute* (Alan Pakula, 1971), *Badlands* (Terence Malick, 1973). So Euro-American art films were not, at this point, swimming against the artistic tides. It is, however, remarkable that so many European art-film directors gained access to American filmmaking.

A possible explanation would be that at this historical moment, the conflicts within American society—the Vietnam War protests, the generation gap, the Black Power movement, the beginnings of modern feminism, the sexual revolution—created a window of opportunity for sympathetic works from European artists. For a few years, European filmmakers had access to American financing and American markets even if they were ideologically opposed to American capitalism. American companies supported a range of socially critical Euro-American projects: *Zabriskie Point, Model Shop, Burn, Last Tango in Paris*. Additionally, European filmmakers joined with American cultural and/or political radicals in a number of collaborations. Joan Baez collaborated with Ennio Morricone on the theme song for the Italian-produced, English-language film *Sacco and Vanzetti*; Bernardo Bertolucci worked with the Living Theater (on *Agonia*, a short film made in 1967), then with Marlon Brando; Jean-Luc Godard began, but never finished, an American film made in collaboration with Richard Leacock and D.A. Pennebaker.

Even within this period of relative openness, however, the possibility of political discourse is limited. Specifically political films (*Burn, Sacco and Vanzetti*, portions of *One Plus One* and *Zabriskie Point*) are rare. Films about lifestyle, individual perception, and the institutions of everyday life are more common (*Lions Love, Model Shop, More, Last Tango in Paris*, the overall perspectives of *One Plus One* and *Zabriskie Point*). Makavejev's *WR* attempts a synthesis of political and sexual issues, but it is essentially a film about sexuality.

Not all Euro-American films of the late 1960s and early 1970s present an atmosphere of rapid social change. *Romeo and Juliet* (1968), directed by Franco Zeffirelli, is a well-made adaptation shot in Verona and featuring two attractive teenagers in the title roles. *Brother Sun, Sister Moon* (1972), also by Zeffirelli, is a handsome historical film about St. Francis with songs by pop star Donovan. *The Trojan Women* (1971), starring Katharine Hepburn and directed by Michael Cacoyannis, is not particularly relevant to the Vietnam War, despite a closing statement which tries to make the connection. *The Touch* (1971), the first English-language film by Ingmar Bergman, has more to do with Bergman's existential themes than with the social movements of the 1960s. Bergman has some problems with point of view, since the English-language filming privileges the Elliott Gould character, whereas the narrative seems more tied to the Swedish couple (Bibi Andersson and Max von Sydow).

Luchino Visconti made three high-budget English-language costume dramas in 1968–1973. *The Damned* (1969) is about self-destruction and mutual destruction within a prominent German family during the Nazi period. Diverse, often cruel, sexuality is shown. *Death in Venice* (1971) is a beautiful, slow-paced adaptation of Thomas Mann's novel, featuring Dirk Bogarde as Aschenbach. Visconti solves the language problem of presenting Venice during tourist season by having several scenes with no dialogue (but with musical accompaniment), and by including some untranslated lines in French, German, Italian, and Polish. *Ludwig* (1973) tells the story of the mad King Ludwig II of Bavaria, who in Visconti's version is not an unstable monster, but a sensitive, artistic young man given to extravagance. All three films describe excesses and irrationalities of the recent European past. That the films have a European, rather than strictly Italian, focus may have been a result of their international financing.

For *Romeo and Juliet, Brother Sun, Sister Moon, The Trojan Women, The Touch,* and the Visconti films, the social changes of the late sixties and early seventies are almost invisible except for somewhat more explicit scenes of sexuality. The movements of the sixties did not affect all sectors of American and Western European society equally; indeed, movies, with their youthful audiences, may tend to exaggerate the importance of the changes. The Visconti films do present images of social instability, but it would be reductive to call these films responses to the 1960s. In *Death in Venice,* for example, Aschenbach's attraction to the boy Tadzio in a city ravaged by cholera has resonances to the passing of nineteenth-century haut bourgeois privilege, to the old age of the filmmaker (Visconti died in 1976), to the philosophical debate of the sensual versus the spiritual, and to Thomas Mann's early-twentieth-

THE TOUCH
Elliot Gould, Bibi Andersson, Max von Sydow, director Ingmar Bergman.

century novella. *Death in Venice* may be responding to the social upheavals of the sixties and the new candor about homosexuality as well. However, unlike many films of the period its social context cannot be limited to a time frame of a few years.

In the mid-1970s, Euro-American art films did not disappear, but they had far less critical and commercial impact than in the previous period. *The Night Porter* (1974), directed by Liliana Cavani, was a minor addition to the socio-psycho-sexual genre represented by *Last Tango in Paris* and *The Damned. Salon Kitty* (alternate title *Madam Kitty*, 1976), an exploitative variation on the same theme, was an enormous commercial success in Italy but a failure in the United States despite a number of English-speaking actors in featured roles. Dusan Makavejev's *Sweet Movie* (1974) intertwines two fictional stories plus documentary footage of a commune practicing primal therapy in a reprise of the themes and techniques of *WR: Mysteries of the Organism.* Francesco Rosi's *Lucky Luciano* (1974) is an interesting mixture of documentary and fiction, exposé and crime film, but its impact on American viewers was muted by its "B" movie cast and atmosphere. Polanski's *The Tenant* (1976) is an inward-looking psychological thriller, consistent with his earlier films but in no sense a new pathway.

Antonioni's *The Passenger* (1975) can be seen as a variation on *Last Tango in Paris*, with Jack Nicholson playing the Brando part of a disillusioned and desperate middle-aged man, and Maria Schneider reprising her role as a free-spirited young woman. But in Antonioni's film the emphasis is not in the bedroom but rather in the male character's giving up of identity and attachments. *The Passenger* also extends *Blow-Up*'s theme of art and reality by considering how a reporter (the Nicholson character) shapes and distorts his journalistic pieces. This lucid existential fable is one of Antonioni's finest films. It had a modestly successful theatrical run in the United States, ranking fourth among foreign films in 1975.

Fellini's ambitious *Casanova* (1976), starring Donald Sutherland, was badly reviewed for its lack of passion, and had a disappointing commercial career. Fellini told Aldo Tassone that after accepting the project, he found nothing sympathetic in the historical Casanova, and therefore he made a film about the emptiness, the void he felt for this character.[11] Fellini's adventurer is foolish, narcissistic, deluded about his own importance. He is so self-involved that a life-sized wooden doll excites him more than a real woman. Fellini's ambivalence about polymorphous sexuality and decadence in *Satyricon* here becomes a clear expression of distaste.

The most controversial Euro-American art film of this period was undoubtedly Bertolucci's *1900* (1976). Lavishly supported by Hollywood companies and featuring a large international cast, *1900* was intended by Bertolucci as a breakthrough work, a commercial feature film that would change people's political sympathies. The strategy of producing a big-budget Marxist film was not completely ludicrous, since in 1969 Hollywood companies had encouraged and supported antiestablishment works. However, by 1976 the moment of social change had ended and the film industry expected business as usual. In this climate, Bertolucci's attempt to make a five-hour-long Marxist film, with lengthy operatic setpieces, was directly contradictory to the aims and needs of the companies that were financing him. The production and release of *1900* degenerated into legal battles between Bertolucci, Grimaldi, Paramount, and Fox, and the film was ultimately released in the United States only in a greatly shortened version. *1900* demonstrated that even the gifted director of *Last Tango in Paris* was not a guaranteed box-office success, and therefore it hurt the commercial credibility of all European art-film directors.

In content as well, *1900* is an equivocal film. Its epic of twentieth-century Italian history as experienced in the countryside near Parma attempts to portray a triumph of the peasantry, but no such triumph is historically available. Bertolucci therefore begins and ends his film with the Liberation of 1945, a brief moment when peasant control and land reform seemed possible. Post-1945 history is presented only in a symbolic epilog. Bertolucci also spends a great deal of time on the personal, often specifically sexual, rivalry of his two heroes, the peasant Olmo (Gérard Depardieu) and the aristocrat Alfredo (Robert De Niro), suggesting themes of doubling and of Oedipal anxiety.[12] By convoluting history and narrative in these ways, Bertolucci creates a sprawling and ultimately rather hermetic film instead of a popular or populist epic.

The lawsuits, censorship battles, and disappointing financial results of *1900* and other films in the mid-1970s forced Alberto Grimaldi to curtail his ambitious production program. Grimaldi canceled a proposed Bertolucci adaptation of Dashiell Hammett's *Red Harvest*, delayed Sergio Leone's epic *Once Upon a Time in America*, and limited his activities to a few low-budget pictures. In 1975–1976 Grimaldi had produced *1900*, *Fellini Casanova*, Pasolini's *Salo*, and Rosi's *Illustrious Corpses*. In 1979–1980 Grimaldi announced a production slate of *Hurricane Rosy*, a French-language film about female wrestlers, and *Letters to the Lovelorn*, a low-budget Italian-language comedy.[13]

The American auteur films of the mid-1970s fared better than their Euro-American counterparts. Some interesting films of the period are *The Conversation* (Francis Coppola, 1974), *Nashville* (Robert Altman, 1975), *Taxi Driver* (Martin Scorsese, 1976), and *Annie Hall*

(Woody Allen, 1977). Diane Jacobs referred to this era of American film as a "Hollywood Renaissance," with only modest hyperbole.[14] But the renaissance was short-lived. In the wake of *Star Wars* (1977), American film quickly became more conservative and more genre-oriented. Emblematic of the change was the iconoclastic Altman's departure from Hollywood in the late 1970s after a series of box-office flops.

Over the next several years (1977–1985), Euro-American films were, in general, marginal to the important commercial and artistic trends in world cinema. Bertolucci's *Luna* (1979), with its central theme of incest, received violently negative reviews and was a commercial failure. Lina Wertmuller's *The End of the World in Our Usual Bed in a Night Full of Rain* (1978) was an unsuccessful attempt to broaden the appeal of her Italian-language films. The stormy cross-cultural marriage between Giancarlo Giannini and Candice Bergen has potential interest; so does the device of using male and female friends—as opposed "Greek choruses"—to comment on the action. But in the English-language version, at least, the characters are undeveloped and the fragmented time scheme is confusing. Claude Lelouch's *Another Man, Another Chance* (1977) was a strange juxtaposition of Paris under siege (during the Franco-Prussian War) and the frontier towns of Texas. It is visually striking but has difficulty integrating these two worlds via a narrative of emigration. Alain Resnais' *Providence* (1977) was a beautiful chamber-cinema film, too refined and intellectual for popular success. Like *The Passenger*, it is a lucid film with a difficult subject—in this case, the immanence of death. Ingmar Bergman's *The Serpent's Egg* (1977) was a disappointing effort from a great filmmaker; Bergman notes in his autobiography that he did not feel comfortable with the Berlin in the 1920s setting.[15] The film tries unconvincingly to tie a mystery plot involving several bizarre deaths to the onset of Nazism. *Death Watch* (Bertrand Tavernier, 1979), *Montenegro* (Dusan Makavejev, 1981), *Tales of Ordinary Madness* (Marco Ferreri, 1981), and *The Coca-Cola Kid* (Makavejev, 1985) are all disappointing English-language films by well-known European directors.

The Greek-born, French-based Constantin Costa-Gavras was one of the few European directors of this period to establish himself as an English-language film director. *Missing* (1982), a well-made film about the right-wing coup in Chile, showed that Costa-Gavras' political melodramas could work in a Hollywood studio context. *Hannah K* (1983), starring Jill Clayburgh, was a thoughtful film about the Israeli-Palestinian conflict. More recently, Costa-Gavras has made *Betrayed* (1988) and *The Music Box* (1989), two English-language films set in the United States.

Louis Malle, another French filmmaker lured to English-language production, moved to the United States and made several films in the late 1970s and early 1980s. *Pretty Baby* (1978), *Atlantic City* (1981), and *My Dinner With André* (1981) are low-budget, character-oriented films which transpose the values of the European art film to American settings. *Crackers* (1984) is a disappointing caper comedy, set in San Francisco. *Alamo Bay* (1985) presents in melodramatic form the conflict between Anglo and Vietnamese shrimpers on the Texas coast. In the late 1980s Malle returned to France to make *Au revoir les enfants* (1988), a film which has an autobiographical element lacking in all of his American work.

France and Italy had been the major art-film producers in continental Europe from 1945 into the 1970s. However, this dominance was challenged in the mid-1970s by the West German filmmakers sometimes referred to as Das Neue Kino. Directors such as Rainer Werner Fassbinder, Werner Herzog, and Wim Wenders gained international prominence, and they quickly turned to the new funding possibilities offered by English-language productions—with widely varying results. Fassbinder's *Despair* (1978) is one of his weaker films—the visual stylization of Fassbinder and the verbal stylization of scriptwriter Tom Stoppard do not mix. Fassbinder's *Querelle* (1982) manages the impressive feat of adapting a play by Jean Genet without softening Genet's intertwined themes of homosexuality and crime. *Querelle* was shot in English but distributed in the United States in a German-language version; this suggests that distributors found it too bizarre for anything but an art-house release.

Werner Herzog's *Stroszek* (1977) involves a German ex-convict and his prostitute girlfriend moving to Wisconsin to start over (the Wisconsin scenes are partially in English). Unfortunately, the change of scene does not change the characters' luck; Herzog does not believe in the United States as the land of the happy ending. *Stroszek* is an intelligent and profoundly sad critique of the American dream. *Fitzcarraldo* (1982) was originally intended as an English-language film starring Jason Robards and Mick Jagger. After a few false starts, Robards and Jagger dropped out and the film was made in German, starring Klaus Kinski. *Where the Green Ants Dream* (1984) is a low-budget film made in Australia about a conflict between aborigines and a mining company. Though indifferently acted and plotted, the film does provide some insights into the worldview of the aborigines.

The German filmmaker most associated with European-American collaborations is Wim Wenders. Wenders' work is specifically about the absence of a positive German culture in the post-Nazi period and the use of American culture as a substitute. Wenders, like many young West

Germans, grew up with American cinema, American rock and roll, even American radio and television (via the Armed Forces Network). He embraced this imported culture while at the same time struggling with the need for a European culture and a European identity. His films are therefore about wanderings from Europe to America and back, encounters with Americans and American culture, searches for personal identity. These themes are central to *Alice in the Cities* (1973), about a German reporter who travels from the United States to Germany and becomes a sort of guardian of a young German girl in the process, and to *The American Friend* (1977), about a shady American entrepreneur (Dennis Hopper) who corrupts an honest German frame-maker (Bruno Ganz). Wenders actually worked in the United States from 1977 to 1984, directing *Hammett* (1982) and *Paris, Texas* (1984). The earlier film, a fiction loosely based on the life of Dashiell Hammett, is not one of Wenders' better films; it had a long and contentious production history marked by interventions from executive producer Francis Coppola. Like *One From the Heart* (1982), Coppola's other major production of this time, *Hammett* features superb art direction but a less-than-satisfactory plot. *Paris, Texas,* on the other hand, is a marvelous film integrating Wenders' themes of wandering and the search for identity with the varied landscapes of the American West (the deserts of West Texas, the cityscapes of Los Angeles and Houston). *Paris, Texas* won the Golden Palm at Cannes in 1984. Wenders has in the late 1980s returned to Germany to work, declaring that "I had in these 7 1/2 years [in America] come to accept myself as a European filmmaker and come to accept myself as a German in my heart."[16] With *Wings of Desire* (1988), Wenders returned to Germany; the film was set in Berlin and shot primarily in German.

Wenders' work is one prominent exception to the generalization that the period 1977–1985 was not kind to the art film. These were the years of optimistic storytelling in the American film industry, represented by the *Star Wars* trilogy and the films of Steven Spielberg. Economically, the American studios made fewer but more expensive films (the "blockbuster" strategy), and distributed them in broad release patterns supported by saturation TV advertising. In terms of content, the new American films stressed simple genre patterns, special effects, and the victory of good over evil. Peter Biskind accuses the enormously popular films of George Lucas and Spielberg, built on adventure stories and special effects, of "infantilizing the audience": they are in favor of children and childhood "innocence," against grownups and adult sexuality.[17] All of these trends negatively affected Euro-American art films, which present adult stories for an adult or young adult audience, not for

'ROUND MIDNIGHT
Bertrand Tavernier directs Dexter Gordon.

Courtesy of the Academy of Motion Picture Arts and Sciences.

the blockbuster audience of "eight to eighty." Also, because they are somewhat specialized, Euro-American art films have difficulty competing with films backed by TV advertising designed to open in 2500 suburban multiplexes.

Nevertheless, in the second half of the 1980s a new flurry of Euro-American art-film productions began. Jean-Jacques Annaud directed *The Name of the Rose* (1986), based on the surprising best-selling novel by Italian semiotician Umberto Eco. This film, which starred Sean Connery, was a hit in Europe, but could not repeat the strong commercial showing of the novel in the United States. Bertrand Tavernier's *'Round Midnight* (1986) was an interesting fictional look at expatriate American jazz musicians. It featured the music of Dexter Gordon (star of the film), Herbie Hancock, and other fine musicians. Two films were made in English about the international world of film production: *Good Morning, Babylon* (1987), by Paolo and Vittorio Taviani, and *A Man in Love* (1987), by Diane Kurys. The first had a wonderful premise—two Italian artisans emigrate to the U.S. and assist in building the sets for D. W. Griffith's *Intolerance* (1916)—but was confusingly plotted. The second was a well-made love story set in the milieu of international film production.

Young French director Luc Besson made *The Big Blue* (1987), a film about the mystical experience of deep-sea diving. This film was enormously successful in France but could not find a public in the United States, where it was mismarketed as an adolescent adventure film. *Julia and Julia* (1987), directed by Peter Del Monte and produced by Italian state television (RAI), was the first feature film shot in High Definition Television and transferred to motion picture stock. Kathleen Turner starred, and an English-language version was made to enhance the film's commercial prospects. Unfortunately, the film's images are often murky, so the HDTV experiment cannot be called a success. *Bagdad Cafe* (1988), a film by director, co-writer, and co-producer Percy Adlon and co-writer and co-producer Eleonore Adlon, is a wonderfully off-beat story about a German woman who discovers a supportive community and a new sense of herself in the tiny "oasis" of Bagdad (a Mojave Desert town). This film was critically and commercially successful in Europe. Though less successful in the United States, it did inspire a short-lived television series.

Other recent Euro-American art films are Barbet Schroeder's *Barfly* (1987), Percy and Eleonore Adlon's *Rosalie Goes Shopping* (1990), Jean-Jacques Annaud's *The Bear* (1989), Uli Edel's *Last Exit to Brooklyn* (1990), Volker Schlondorff's *The Handmaid's Tale* (1990), Bernardo Bertolucci's *The Sheltering Sky* (1990), Wim Wenders' *Until the End of the*

World (1991), and Lasse Hallstrom's *Once Around* (1991). Doris Dorrie's English-language comedy *Me and Him* (1988) and Francesco Rosi's film *The Palermo Connection* (1989) have appeared in the United States only on videocassette. Still to be released in the U.S. are *Confessions of a Holy Drinker* (Ermanno Olmi, 1988), *St. Francis* (Liliana Cavani, 1989), *I Want to Go Home* (Alain Resnais, 1989), and *Voyager* (Volker Schlondorff, 1991).

Certainly the most extraordinary Euro-American film of recent years is Bernardo Bertolucci's *The Last Emperor* (1987). This is a big-budget English-language film shot in China by a primarily Italian crew. It was produced by Englishman Jeremy Thomas and financed by a consortium of European banks, based on distribution guarantees from European and Japanese distributors. The film combines psychological insight with epic sweep in telling the story of Pu Yi, the last Manchu emperor, who ended his days as a gardener in the People's Republic of China. *The Last Emperor* was critically acclaimed and had an extremely strong commercial career in Europe and Japan. In the United States the film won nine Academy Awards and had a good, though not overwhelming, theatrical run.

The Last Emperor is actually a Euro-American-Asian film, since it was made with the assistance of the People's Republic of China and it involves Japanese participation (in acting and music, for example) as well. The collaboration with Asia has a precedent in the Jeremy Thomas-produced *Merry Christmas, Mr. Lawrence* (1983), directed by Nagisa Oshima. This film about British internees in a Japanese prison camp is a powerful study of the conflict between Western and Japanese moral codes. It achieved a "succès d'estime," but did not have the worldwide impact of *The Last Emperor*. The latter film benefited from an infatuation with all things Chinese during the late 1980s, when a modernizing People's Republic opened its doors to Western businessmen, intellectuals, and tourists. Today, in the wake of the Tienamen Square massacres, the reception of a film about modern China would probably be quite different.

The Last Emperor, like many Euro-American films of the late 1980s, was financed by European sources rather than by the American studios. *Good Morning, Babylon, A Man in Love, Julia and Julia, The Bear*, and *Paris, Texas* are examples of the same trend. This is quite different from the situation of the 1960s, when American companies were financing English-language films made in Europe by Europeans. Today the American studios are not particularly interested in supporting European-made prestige pictures; they are doing very well with American-made comedies and adventures. The large European production companies (e.g., Gaumont) or television networks (e.g., RAI) are turning to English-language production as a last resort because ambitious projects in French, Italian, or German will have difficulty earning back their costs. From a cultural point of view, this can reach levels of absurdity, with European governments supporting films in English in the name of safeguarding cultural autonomy. From a commercial point of view, the move to English-language filming is also risky, since the existence of an English-language version does not guarantee North American or worldwide distribution. However, the European companies seem to have few options. Either they invest in English-language filming, or they cede the worldwide business of filmmaking to the American major studios. Given this stark choice, the move to English-language films by European producers will probably continue.

BAGDAD CAFE
The warm, caring community.

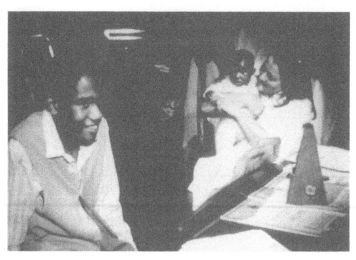

5. Cultural Dominance or Cultural Mix

It should be evident by this point that a multinational but English-language cinema has been a part of European and American film production for at least the last thirty years, and that this Euro-American cinema is a prominent part of world cinema today. The current chapter explores the implications of the shift from films that are culturally and linguistically "national" to Euro-American, cross-cultural films. Is this shift an instance of cultural imperialism, of American film dominating and supplanting the film cultures of other nations? Is there a cultural mix going on, a two-way flow of influence? Or is some combination of these two hypotheses (domination plus mix) the most adequate description of Euro-American film?

As a preliminary step, let us note that the dominance of the English language in world film production (excluding Asia) is not an isolated phenomenon. In the second half of the twentieth century, English has become a worldwide language of science, technology, business, politics, and entertainment. Scientific conferences around the world are conducted in English. Air-traffic controllers use English as an international language. Diplomatic and commercial negotiations are often conducted in English, even if it is the primary language of none of those concerned. English-language journals, both popular and scholarly, have worldwide circulations. And the newest words of technology and leisure are often coined in English and then absorbed by other languages, e.g., il computer, le weekend.

Jeremy Tunstall and Stewart Brand see the rise of English as a world language as a consequence of British power in the nineteenth century and American power in the twentieth.[1] The British Empire spread the English language to North America, India, Africa, Australia, the Caribbean, and so on. Then American economic and military power in the mid-twentieth century, a period of rapid advancement in transportation and communication, brought the language to the four corners of the world. In an era of accelerated change, the use of a standard language for science and technology is extremely helpful. International trade also requires a standard language that can be used by trading partners with widely diverse primary languages. Because of American dominance in the post–World War II period, English has been the chosen language.

There is also a cultural explanation for the pre-eminence of English. In his futuristic novel *A Clockwork Orange* (1963), Anthony Burgess speculated that a Russian slang would seep into the language of Great Britain. Burgess's premonition was that Russian socialism and Russian culture would spread to other nations. It fact, it is American culture which has permeated the world. Blue jeans, American movies, and rock and roll have circumnavigated the globe, and McDonald's has arrived in Moscow. American popular culture presents an image of personal freedom and material opportunity to audiences around the world. In doing so, the popular culture of today builds on two centuries of European and American literature and legend portraying the United States as a promised land. The image carried by cultural channels may not correspond in all respects to American reality, but still the dream of the United States as a land of opportunity retains its potency.

The existence of Euro-American films—of European films made in English—is thus one aspect of a broader invasion of the English language and of American culture. As with the broader invasion, the reshaping of European film to approximate American models has both economic and cultural dimensions. Economically, the use of the English language gives a French, or Italian, or German film at least a potential access to the American market and to American-controlled world distribution. The adherence to American models also lessens the competitive strength of non-English-language film industries, especially since it is often the most talented filmmakers who are attracted to big-budget, English-language filming. Culturally, English-language filming often carries the ideological baggage of American values—materialism, individualism, etc. Key characteristics of the Hollywood film such as spectacle, entertainment, and the star system may be the stylistic equivalents of such values. So, the Euro-American art film is an instance of dominance, or more precisely of hegemony. I take this term from the Italian Marxist theorist Antonio Gramsci (1891–1937), who explains the stability of European capitalist states in the early twentieth century by distinguishing between rule by force and rule by cultural adherence.[2] In the latter pattern, which Gramsci calls "hegemony," individuals accept the authority of the state because it is part of a larger cultural fabric of traditions, beliefs, institutions, artifacts, and experiences. This cultural hegemony is ideologically distorted, but it does serve human needs to a certain extent, so that in stable social-political conditions hegemonic values are not questioned. Recognizing the importance and the power of hegemony, Gramsci called not for its destruction, but for the creation of a "counter hegemony" which would advocate a new set of values.[3]

Although Gramsci's cultural interests were primarily literary, and he paid scant attention to cinema, he did describe a specific instance of cross-cultural influence of direct relevance to the interactions of European and American film. Why, Gramsci asked, was there no Italian popular literature, and why was nineteenth-century French literature (for example, the works of Alexandre Dumas) so popular in Italy? He found that French popular literature appealed to a broad spectrum of the bourgeoisie and the working class (a "historical bloc" in Gramsci's terminology), and that there was no equivalent literature in Italy.[4] Italian intellectuals, according to Gramsci, had not found a way "to elaborate a modern 'humanism' able to reach right to the simplest and most uneducated classes."[5] This corresponded to a political situation in which French republicanism responded to at least some of the needs of the popular classes, whereas a fragmented and confused Italian politics did not. Gramsci specifically described the influence of French popular literature as "the moral and intellectual hegemony of foreign intellectuals."[6]

Gramsci's cross-cultural analysis of literature has its analogy in film history, where European cinema has traditionally appealed to an upper-middle-class audience and American cinema to a broad range of classes.[7] Herbert Gans and James Monaco, writing twenty years apart, both point to the narrow class appeal of European film and the much broader worldwide appeal of American film.[8] European films tend to be elitist in style and frame of reference even when they have a specifically left-wing orientation. In American cinema, action-genre films appealing to an international working-class audience have been produced steadily for eighty years.

Gramsci was not satisfied by the importation of popular culture from France. He wished to build a "national-popular" culture in Italy, representing a broad class alliance and responding to specifically Italian problems. The analogy with European cinema becomes a bit strained here, because Gramsci wanted a popular culture that would legitimize a Marxist revolutionary movement. European filmmakers and governments have a range of reasons, both economic and cultural, for seeking lively national-popular cultures. In many cases these reasons are not revolutionary, but instead are conservative, seeking to sustain a national identity. But I think that European filmmakers and policy-makers would agree that an imported popular culture is not sufficient. Even if that culture brings with it some positive values, it cannot address with any specificity the problems and potentials of the importing society.

To return to our specific subject, Euro-American films have a bicultural or multicultural orientation. Therefore, in many cases they will enact the "hegemony of foreign intellectuals," or of a foreign popular culture, instead of being rooted in the social and cultural life of a single nation. The frustrations of making bicultural films in an economic situation dominated by American cinema are described by Francesco Rosi: "This market [the Italian market for motion pictures circa 1980] demands tremendous adaptability, such as being able to film a story in a language different from that of its cultural place of origin, or winking exclusively at the possible agreements of a market, different in culture and tradition, with the result, in most cases however, that one no longer knows who one is or what one is saying."[9]

But if there is a hegemonic influence of American film on European film, there is also an influence in the other direction. The European art film has influenced American film on at least two levels. First, the success of the European art film in the 1960s had a broad influence on how American filmmakers conceptualized cinema and on the films they produced. It was a fairly common sentiment in the 1960s that the new ideas in film were coming from Europe. *Saturday Review* in 1960 devoted a special section to the topic "Are Foreign Films Better?"[10] Peter Bart of the *New York Times* wrote feature articles in the mid-1960s on the decline of Hollywood and the impact of European film.[11] Further, the auteur theory of Truffaut and Godard has strongly influenced American filmmakers since the 1960s. American would-be auteurs have often borrowed rather explicitly from Europe. Paul Schrader, scriptwriter for *Taxi Driver* and now a well-established writer-director, wrote a book on three art-film directors—Dreyer, Bresson, and Ozu. Schrader's films combine visual elements of Bresson and Ozu with genre-based story structures. Woody Allen's debt to Ingmar Bergman is visible in *Interiors* and *Hannah and Her Sisters,* among other films. Allen's work can be seen as a struggle between comedy elements and the psychological and philosophical issues raised by Bergman. Francis Coppola in the 1970s professed an admiration for Bernardo Bertolucci: "He's an extraordinary talent. I look at two reels of *The Conformist* every day. He's my freedom therapy."[12] Following up on this admiration, Coppola has worked with Bertolucci's gifted cameraman Vittorio Storaro on several films (*Apocalypse Now,* 1978; *One from the Heart,* 1982; *Tucker,* 1988; *New York Stories,* 1989). Coppola has also made one film that is very close to art-film models—*The Conversation* (1974), which shows the influence of Bertolucci and Antonioni.

In the 1980s and 1990s, it is particularly the visual elements of European cinema that have found their way to American film. The leading European cinematographers have become successful and in demand in the United States, whereas narrative and philosophical concepts have been more difficult to import. Aside from Storaro, Sven Nyqvist (long-time collaborator of Bergman), Robbie Muller (cinematographer for Wenders), and Nestor Almendros (cinematographer for Truffaut and Eric Rohmer, among others) have established themselves as top cine-matographers for American film. Their intelligence, their artistry with natural light, their contribution to a directorial concept are enormously valued.[13]

A second level of influence can be seen in the hybrid, Euro-American films that are my central concern. Euro-American art films are attempts at a synthesis. They involve a recognition of the intelligence and emotional power of European filmmaking, and an effort to reshape that intelligence and power into a format accessible to American audiences. American film often plays the leading role in such attempts, but European film also contributes to the shape of this new, hybrid form. The exact nature of the synthesis varies from film to film. *Hammett* is a collaborative project shaped by executive producer Francis Coppola, four American scriptwriters, and production designer Dean Tavoularis as well as by Wenders. *Satyricon,* on the other hand, is stylistically, thematically, and technically a film by Fellini and his usual collabora-tors (e.g., scriptwriter Bernardino Zappone, editor Ruggero Mastroianni, composer Nino Rota) which happens to exist in an English-language version because of international marketing considerations.

Often Euro-American films are specifically about a mix of Ameri-can and European cultures. Sometimes the intersection of Americans and Europeans is presented in a pro-American way. In *Bagdad Cafe,* for example, Jasmin escapes from a cold, formal relationship with her hus-band to find a warm, caring community in the American desert town of Bagdad. Often, though, Euro-American films are critical of Americans and American culture. In *Contempt,* the brutal and bombastic Ameri-can producer, Jeremy Prokosch, is compared unfavorably to the courtly European director, Fritz Lang. In *Burn,* the British agent, Sir William Walker (played by American actor Marlon Brando), manipulates a slave revolution for his government's ends, and later supervises the hunting down of the revolutionaries he himself had trained. In *1900,* American star Robert De Niro is cast as the weak landowner who cooperates with the Fascists, whereas French actor Gérard Depardieu gets the heroic role of the peasant, Olmo.

How does one account for the influence of European culture on a hegemonic American culture in the film industry, a stronghold of American media power? A thorough answer to this question would in-volve economics, politics, audience-study, and cultural analysis. If we

L'ECLISSE
The anomie of women.

limit ourselves to culture, the question can be answered by three somewhat contradictory explanations. First, the art film can be seen as a survival of an earlier cultural hegemony, a remnant of the dominance of Western Europe over the United States. From this point of view, art films are valued as part of a prestigious high culture, along with opera and literary "classics." This kind of backward-looking culture has an influence, but it is confined to a relatively small audience.

A second explanation would point to American-rooted institutions of film culture as broadening the appeal of the art film. Such innovations as film schools, film festivals, and the more serious film criticism of the 1960s (represented by Pauline Kael and Andrew Sarris, among others) created an increasing sensitivity to films outside the Hollywood norms. The audiences molded by these institutions supported both Hollywood and European films. Stanley Kauffmann, writing in 1966, spoke of these audiences as "the Film Generation," a group of well-educated young people who looked to film for their most important artistic experiences.[14]

A third, content-oriented explanation would say that art films provide a forum for new and challenging ideas. European art films were popular with American audiences of the late 1950s and early 1960s in part because they called attention to what was missing in American cultural products of the time. They challenged the status quo optimism of Hollywood films in the 1950s not by direct attack, but by posing new problems. *L'Avventura* (1959), *L'Eclisse* (1962), and *Red Desert* (1964) by Antonioni, for example, used female protagonists to describe the anomie of consumerism and of separation from productive activity. *Breathless*, the first feature by Godard, and *The Four Hundred Blows*, the first feature by Truffaut, described the estrangement of young people from established values. This third argument suggests that art films were perceived as "better" than American films because of their implicit social criticisms.

Despite an apparent contradiction, all three explanations are correct. Art films embody the prestige of traditional high art; art films also respond to social problems unperceived by the majority culture. Conservative and progressive appeals can coexist in the same cultural phenomenon. But it seems clear that only the second and third appeals—the linkage between new audiences and new subject matter—can explain the art film's expanding influence in the 1960s and 1970s.

Continuing with the third explanation, we can see that art films became more important as their criticisms became matters of greater concern. The late 1960s in the United States was a period of social ferment marked by a loss of confidence in traditional values and by an outburst of social movements and ideas (the New Left, the hippie counterculture, minority activism, the ecology movement, feminism, gay liberation). A Gramscian description of the period would say that hegemony was challenged by a number of emergent social groups, acting sometimes alone, sometimes in collaboration. In terms of cultural activity, the period of roughly 1968–1973 was marked by a tremendous diversity of new ideas and styles, responding to the uncertainties and conflicts of social life. And as part of this diversity, European filmmakers were able to participate in the wave of social criticism which they had to some extent prefigured.

Despite a striking convergence of vocabulary ("counter hegemony" and "counterculture"), I am reluctant to call the social and cultural ferment of the late 1960s a Gramscian counter hegemony. Gramsci, a leader of the Italian Communist Party until his imprisonment in 1926, thought that challenges to hegemony should coalesce around the leadership of a class (e.g., the proletariat) manifested by the political and cultural activities of a political party. The late 1960s in the United States, by contrast, was a disorganized, largely spontaneous period of social change, and its challenge to dominant values was quickly diffused. Following a distinction made by Raymond Williams, I would say that the "alternative or oppositional initiatives and contributions" of the period were, on balance, absorbable within hegemony rather than being "irreducible" or "independent" initiatives.[15] Nevertheless, this period did produce incremental changes and a brief vista of alternate social possibilities. Both the practical changes and the visionary new possibilities are presented in some Euro-American films.

The Gramscian argument of a period of rapid social change providing an opening for European filmmakers seems less applicable to the late 1980s and early 1990s, which is the second period of flowering of the Euro-American art film. For the films of this later period (*'Round Midnight, Barfly, A Man in Love, The Big Blue, Bagdad Cafe, The Last Emperor, Until the End of the World*, etc.), less American capital is involved. Instead of cooperating with American companies, European production companies are making English-language films of their own. The Euro-American films of 1986–1992 can be interpreted to some degree as desperate efforts of European producers to stay alive by imitating American models. Two examples from France, the West European country most identified with resistance to American cultural invasion, can suggest the desperation with which the Europeans have embraced English-language film culture. In 1989, the Ministry of Culture announced that English-language films would in some cases qualify for the state aid reserved for films of French nationality. Also in 1989, a lavish two-part version of *The French Revolution* was produced, with French- and English-language versions, a thoroughly international cast, and an American director for part two. The latter example is particularly strange, because the Euro-American conditions of production would seem to negate the celebration of nationalism which is desired.

However, a more positive interpretation can also be cast on the Euro-American films of the last few years. In a period of waning American economic and political influence, the use of the English language may not be identical to a submission to American power. As English becomes more and more a world language, it may become less identified with the interests of the United States and Great Britain. It seems very likely that English will be a major language, and perhaps even the primary language, of filmed entertainment produced in the European Economic Community in the 1990s. But such film and television programming may nevertheless develop a perspective which varies in some respects from American models. Several of the Euro-American films of the last few years have been strong, in some cases enormous, successes in Europe, but only moderately successful in the United States. Examples would include *The Name of the Rose*, *The Big Blue*, and even *The Last Emperor*, which despite its Academy Awards was only a moderate commercial success in the United States, but was the most popular film of the year in Italy. Perhaps European-made English-language films, instead of catering to the needs of the American market, are beginning to develop a distinctively European perspective. This change in emphasis is certainly not a Gramscian counter hegemony, but it may indicate a shift toward a more European-centered international film industry.

Recent moves by Japanese companies in the field of film financing suggest a further complication of international cinema. With Sony's purchase of Columbia Pictures, Matsushita's purchase of MCA, Japanese participation in films produced by Jeremy Thomas, JVC's financing of *Mystery Train* (a low-budget film by Jim Jarmusch), and a number of other arrangements completed or under discussion, it is clear that Japanese companies will be heavily involved at least in the economic side of international, English-language film production. To what extent will their economic involvement affect the kinds of films that are made? The examples of *Merry Christmas, Mr. Lawrence* and of *Mystery Train* (in which two of the main characters are Japanese teenagers on a "pilgrimage" to the rock and roll sights of Memphis, Tennessee) suggest that a Japanese cultural influence will play a part in Asian-American or Euro-Asian-American cinema.

In the relationship between American and European film industries there seems to be a hegemony *and* a two-way flow of influence.

The economic power and cultural appeal of American film are certainly behind the trend towards English-language filmmaking in Western European film industries. But there is a surprising influence in the other direction as well: the European art film has had an impact on American filmmaking. Hegemony and two-way influence actually seem to coexist in some aspects of the Euro-American art film.

Consider, for example, the "recruitment" of European art-film directors to English-language production. The signing of European directors to Hollywood contracts was quite common in the 1960s and 1970s. Although it is still going on today, art-film directors are also being signed to make English-language, European-financed films. Whatever the source of financing, the recruitment of a European art-film director for an English-language film can be seen as a gain for an American-dominated international cinema and a loss for the national film industries of Western Europe. English-language production has much to offer a West European director: a large production budget, an analogously large salary, a chance to work with internationally popular stars, access to international distribution. The choice may even be between an English-language film and nothing, since films are expensive and chancy investments and even the most prestigious art-film director may be unemployed for long periods. However, in making an English-language film, a West European director risks the uprootedness described by Rosi.

But the director's recruitment is also a recognition of talent, and a way to display that talent before a larger audience. In most cases a European filmmaker is not signed to make a strictly American film. An Antonioni or a Wenders is signed because of an affinity between director and material and is expected to add a personal slant to the film. Often the director has written or co-written the script, with English-language filming called for because of budget or subject (or both). And the films made in this way are often cross-cultural in subject as well as in production conditions.

Wim Wenders is a good example of a filmmaker who has done impressive work in a cross-cultural situation. Wenders scores his films with American rock and roll while at the same time worrying about questions of cultural identity. "The Yanks have colonized our subconscious," says a character in Wenders' *Kings of the Road* (a German-language film). In recognizing this colonization, Wenders becomes a critical filmmaker working in a cross-cultural situation, and not simply a participant in cultural hegemony. Hegemony still shapes his work and its reception; but hegemony does not entirely close off the possibility of original, between-cultures, artistic expression.

Following up on the Wenders example, I would argue that the mix of cultures in Euro-American films is not always an evasion of Western European social realities, that in many cases it corresponds to a current social reality of great importance. European and American cultures are colliding and mixing in numerous ways. Americans and Europeans are interacting in business, technology, diplomacy, defense, education, the media, tourism, and other fields. Coca-Cola is part of the European landscape. Benetton, an Italian company, has numerous shops in the United States. Popular culture is "colonizing the subconscious." Wenders, Antonioni, Godard, Bertolucci, and other filmmakers are responding artistically and critically to this ongoing process of cultural interaction.

Colin MacCabe, in an excellent article on the "global context" of English literature, suggests that in the twentieth century a once-ethnocentric English culture has become the site of conflicts between "competing and incompatible collectivities," and that this process "reaches right down to the individual riven by contradictions." He gives Joyce as an example of an English writer who is also an Irish writer and a European writer, and whose work expresses the contradictions of these three identities. MacCabe finds that English language and literature have been positively changed by outsiders to such a degree that contemporary English literature "is above all a literature of decolonization from Joyce and Yeats to Rushdie and Lessing."[16]

"Decolonization" is undoubtedly too strong a word to use for Euro-American films. In comparison to literature, film is more committed to a single, mainstream approach (Hollywood cinema) and less open to contrary currents. However, the trend toward bicultural or multicultural art which exhibits and builds from its own contradictions is evident in cinema as well as in literature. Godard once declared himself an "American filmmaker in exile," giving homage to the centrality of the American tradition of filmmaking while at the same time carefully stating his distance from Hollywood.[17] Bertolucci described himself as a "French filmmaker, who had been able to make films not only in Italy but finally in America" (this, incidentally, is a good description of the triple "nationality" of *Last Tango in Paris*).[18] The best Euro-American filmmakers have made creative use of the contradictions between American economic and cultural power and European social and cultural needs.

Cultural hegemony is not, however, a misperception or a dead issue. It influences how films are made and received both at the level of yearly production and distribution figures and at the level of individual films and filmmakers. Quantitatively, the "flow" of film and television programming between the United States and Western Europe heavily favors the United States. Europe imports thousands of hours of film and television programming from the United States each year, whereas American movie theaters and television stations depend almost exclusively on domestically produced programming. At the level of individual films, production and distribution decisions based on the conventions of American cinema and on the needs of the American market still have an enormous influence on what films are made and what films are viewed. For example, Antonioni may be an esteemed art-film director, but he was able to make *Blow-Up* and *The Passenger* only because his producers—Carlo Ponti and MGM—thought these films had a good chance of success in the international (American-dominated) market. Antonioni has published scripts for other film projects which producers and financiers were unwilling to back.[19]

Cultural hegemony exists. But in the specific domain of the Euro-American art film, there has been a two-way flow of influence: from the United States to Western Europe, from Western Europe to the United States. This two-way flow has affected the ways movies are both produced and received in the United States and Western Europe. The two-way flow has also been embodied in a number of stimulating and provocative cross-cultural films.

Part II: Case Studies

Introduction

Part 1 of this book outlined my hypothesis that the Euro-American art film is an important form of international filmmaking. It provided some definitions as well as a history stretching back to 1946. Part 1 did not, however, present an opportunity for a detailed examination of individual films. Even within the history section, the overall shape of the partial merging of the European art film and the American entertainment film took precedence over the analysis of particular films.

In the "Case Studies" which form the second part of the book, I give detailed analyses of five films: *Contempt* (1963), *Blow-Up* (1966), *The Canterbury Tales* (1972), *Paris, Texas* (1984), and *The Last Emperor* (1987). These five films are in a number of ways exemplary of the body of films discussed in Part 1. For one thing, these films involve the collaboration, in a variety of combinations, between American and Western European filmmakers and companies. All of the major film-producing countries of Western Europe—France, Great Britain, Italy, and West Germany—are represented by at least one film. In terms of period, *Contempt, Blow-Up*, and *The Canterbury Tales* exemplify the first major period of Euro-American art films, when American companies invested heavily in English-language, European-based films by art-film directors. *Paris, Texas* and *The Last Emperor* represent the more recent development of English-language films financed by European companies trying to break into the international market. The twelve-year gap (1972–1984) between *The Canterbury Tales* and *Paris, Texas* is not coincidental. This was a period of gradual decline for Euro-American films and for European film in general, a period when world cinema was dominated by blockbuster films from the United States.

The directors of the five case-study films—Jean-Luc Godard, Michelangelo Antonioni, Pier Paolo Pasolini, Wim Wenders, and Bernardo Bertolucci—are surely among the most prominent art-film directors of the post–World War II period. There is some variation, however, in the relationship between these directors and the Euro-American art film. Antonioni, Wenders, and Bertolucci have each made long-term commitments to English-language filming, whereas English-language films have been marginal to the careers of Godard and Pasolini. There is also some variation in the relationship between directors and producers. *Contempt* was marked by a conflict between director and producers. *Blow-Up*, *Canterbury Tales*, and *The Last Emperor* are often analyzed as director's films, but they also fit the production programs of strong, internationally-oriented producers: Carlo Ponti for *Blow-Up*, Alberto Grimaldi for *The Canterbury Tales*, Jeremy Thomas for *The Last Emperor*. *Paris, Texas* seems to be very much a Wim Wenders film, with producers Chris Sievernich and Don Guest assisting the director.

The subject matter of Euro-American art films is tremendously varied. However, in my five-film sample one can find several themes that recur in other Euro-American films. *Contempt* and *Paris, Texas* are two of the many Euro-American art films that comment on America and Americans (see also *La dolce vita*, *Lions Love*, *The American Friend*, *The Coca-Cola Kid*). *Contempt* is a film about cross-cultural misunderstanding and frustration (see *Paisan*, *Breathless*, *The Sheltering Sky*). *Blow-Up* is an early youth-culture film, a response to changes in music, fashion, and mores in the 1960s. Other Euro-American youth-culture films from the same few years (1966–1971) include *Lions Love*, *Model Shop*, *More*, *Zabriskie Point*, and *One Plus One*. *Blow-Up* and *The Canterbury Tales* present social alternatives to the mainstream of American and Western European life, and thus implicitly criticize that mainstream. *Fellini Satyricon*, *Burn*, and *Bagdad Cafe* employ this same device. *The Last Emperor* presents a non-Western society interacting with European and/or American culture; *Merry Christmas, Mr. Lawrence* and *Where the Green Ants Dream* also take this approach. The emphasis on sexuality in *The Canterbury Tales* is certainly representative not only of the Grimaldi films (*Last Tango in Paris*, *Fellini Satyricon*), but also of a large number of Euro-American films of the 1960s and 1970s (e.g., *The Damned*, *La dolce vita*, *More*, *The Night Porter*, *Pretty Baby*, *Repulsion*). This theme seems to be period-specific: the link between "art film" and "sex film" plays an important role in *Contempt*, *Blow-Up*, and *The Canterbury Tales*, but is less relevant to *Paris, Texas* and *The Last Emperor*.

All five of the sample films draw in some way on traditions of high art and culture. *The Canterbury Tales* and *Contempt* (with its subtext of *The Odyssey*) have roots in classical literature. *Blow-Up* and *Contempt* are adaptations of modern literary works, and *Paris, Texas* is based on an original script by playwright Sam Shepard. *The Last Emperor*, the least literary of the five films, is a high culture work in its historical analysis and its exploration of a non-Western society. Not every Euro-American art film makes explicit reference to high culture (for example, *Bagdad Cafe* does not), but such a reference is an effective way to alert audiences to a film's artistic ambitions.

In terms of quality, the sample of five films taken from more than one hundred mentioned in Chapter 4 is clearly skewed towards the most original and most successful works. Sample chapters on *Fahrenheit 451*, *The Serpent's Egg*, *A Night Full of Rain*, *Death Watch*, and *Good Morning, Babylon* instead of the five films chosen would have led to an emphasis on the pitfalls and weaknesses of Euro-American hybrid films. However, my five choices were not the only excellent films available. *Voyage to Italy*, *Repulsion*, *Fellini Satyricon*, *Last Tango in Paris*, *The Passenger*, and *Bagdad Cafe* could just as easily have been selected. I chose five of the works which most successfully synthesize Europe and Hollywood, art and industry in order to explore the creative possibilities of Euro-American films.

CONTEMPT
Brigitte Bardot, Jack Palance, Georgia Moll.

6. Art and Commerce in *Contempt*

Contempt (French title: *Le Mépris*; Italian title: *Il disprezzo*; 1963) is one of several Euro-American art films made to capitalize on the worldwide success of the European art film in the early 1960s. It is at the same time a philosophical and personal film by Jean-Luc Godard, probably the leading art-film director of his generation, and a thoroughly commercial enterprise in international cinema undertaken by three successful producers, Carlo Ponti, Georges de Beauregard, and Joseph E. Levine. But *Contempt* did not effortlessly achieve the synthesis between the art film and Hollywood; it was marked by disagreements between director and producers concerning immediate problems and overall concepts of cinema. What is more, the disagreements clearly mark both the film text itself and its distribution in Western Europe and the United States. A study of *Contempt* can therefore show how conflicting concepts of cinema can alter a film and affect its "history," from preproduction to videocassette release.

Contempt was Jean-Luc Godard's first attempt at large-scale international filmmaking. Godard had signed a contract for one film with Carlo Ponti on the strength of the notoriety of such films as *Breathless* (1959) and *Vivre sa vie* (1962). Godard and Ponti then had trouble agreeing on a subject until Godard discovered that Brigitte Bardot, by then a world-famous "sex symbol," was interested in working with him. With Bardot's participation as an assurance of commercial potential, Godard and Ponti quickly agreed on an adaptation of Alberto Moravia's novel *Il disprezzo* (English title: *A Ghost at Noon*), to be shot in Rome and Capri. [1] The project was to be an Italian-French-American co-production, with Georges de Beauregard as the French producer, Ponti as the Italian producer, and Joe Levine's Embassy Pictures providing most of the budget and guaranteeing American distribution. Filming would be in color and widescreen, which by this time were common in American movies but not in European production. To help the film in the United States, an American star, Jack Palance, was added. Levine was given world distribution rights minus Italy (retained by Ponti) and France (sold to the distribution company Cocinor). All ingredients were now in place for a film that could be attractively marketed in at least three major countries.

However, the various participants in the production of *Contempt* had strikingly different attitudes and objectives. Godard's first films were a part of the French New Wave, a movement of artistically ambitious low-budget films. He was attracted by *Contempt's* one million dollar budget[2] and international stars, but he also wanted to maintain his identity as an art-film director. The plot of *Contempt* can be interpreted in part as an account of Godard's mixed feelings about making a big-budget international film. Bardot in 1963 was extremely dissatisfied with the life of a movie star. She wanted recognition as an actress, and she was excited to be working with Godard.[3] Ponti and Levine, partners in a number of large-scale productions, were individually and collectively aiming to establish themselves as major international producers. Ponti was an expert in Europe-based production, whereas Levine's strength was international distribution. Both men wanted to produce highly commercial films that could be worldwide hits. De Beauregard, a producer associated with the French New Wave, was trying to extend the success of that phenomenon to big-budget, mass-audience films. Though De Beauregard spoke confidently, before production of *Contempt,* about "the sharp, personalized filmmaking concepts of Godard" being "wedded to important box-office values,"[4] the participants' widely diverging goals were at least potentially problematic.

Beyond individual objectives, two distinct concepts of cinema can be discerned in the production of *Contempt.* Godard was committed to film as the expression of an artistic personality. One of the original theorists of the "politique des auteurs," he strongly believed in directorial control. Levine and Ponti, on the other hand, were committed to the formulae of large-scale commercial filmmaking: high production values, well-known stars, familiar genres, heavy doses of sex and/or violence. Levine and Ponti ultimately believed in productorial control, especially during pre-production and post-production. Bardot and De Beauregard were mediating figures, Bardot the major star who wanted recognition as an actress, De Beauregard the producer who wanted to wed commerce and art.

A conflict between writer-director Godard and producers Ponti and Levine was already visible during the scriptwriting process. Godard was not in the habit of writing detailed scripts. For *Breathless,* he had used a story outline by François Truffaut plus a few pages of handwritten notes. For later films, his "scripts" consisted of scribbled notes and drawings, which were constantly altered as production evolved. But *Contempt,* with its substantial budget and international cast, required a fleshed-out script. Therefore, Godard wrote a 104-page script, including 31 pages of character sketches and production notes.[5] However, for one crucial scene of the film, the thirty-minute discussion/argument between Bardot and Michel Piccoli in their apartment, Godard wrote a three-page parenthesis to his "chers Producteurs" in lieu of script pages. This parenthetical note states that Godard, "unlike the directors who win Oscars in Hollywood," cannot imagine the details of an action until he sees the actors and the sets or locations. He cannot describe "Brigitte Bardot taking a bath . . . or the colors of the bathtowel she wraps herself in . . . until after finding them, that is to say after filming them."[6] This elegant disclaimer suggests that Godard was under some pressure to write a detailed script in standard (masterscene) form, and that he found the process frustrating. Carlo Ponti must have been frustrated as well, because he needed a full script for budgeting and scheduling.

The story of *Contempt*, as written and filmed by Godard, has two main foci. It is, first, an account of an international co-production of *The Odyssey* undertaken by producer Jeremy Prokosch (Palance) and director Fritz Lang (playing himself). Prokosch recruits writer Paul Javal (Michel Piccoli) to revise the script. Javal takes the job because he needs money but finds that it creates both professional conflicts—should he side with the courtly and intellectual Lang or the crude but financially dominant Prokosch?—and a rift with his wife Camille (Brigitte Bardot). The widening gap between Paul and Camille is the film's second focus. Camille never fully articulates her reasons for falling out of love with Paul, but they seem to be based on the way Paul allows Prokosch to court her, and more generally on Paul's indecision in his dealings with Prokosch and Lang. Camille eventually runs away with the forceful Prokosch, and the two of them are killed in a car crash. Paul then leaves the film location in Capri to return to Rome, while Lang carries on with the film.

In its broad outlines this is a melodramatic and commercial subject, full of conflict and spectacle. However, in the details of story and mise en scène (many of them unscripted) Godard sabotages the melodrama and substitutes a far more complex set of interests. The several excerpts shown of *The Odyssey* are static and confused rather than spectacular. But *The Odyssey* also serves as the focus of an intellectual debate, with Fritz Lang defending the wholeness and nobility of Homer's world, Prokosch demanding a psychological melodrama, and Paul leaning toward Prokosch's view and seeing in *The Odyssey* a reflection of his own personal problems. This debate has resonances both to the world of cinema—it shows how ideas are inextricably tied to the power relationships between filmmakers—and to the philosophical question of man's connection to God, or the gods. On the latter point, even Fritz Lang cannot reproduce the closeness of man to God in Homer's epic;

his gods are statues with blank, painted eyes, and he approvingly quotes Hölderlin on the "absence of God."

As to the love story, Godard cools the melodrama by presenting the conflict between Paul and Camille almost entirely in conversation, and by showing very little of the developing relationship between Camille and Prokosch. Bardot does have several nude scenes, but these are static, formally manipulated, and separated from the main line of action. The love story is also explicitly paralleled to *The Odyssey*, with Paul as Odysseus, Camille as Penelope, and Prokosch as Poseidon. In the film's ironic retelling of the story, Paul is an anti-Odysseus who loses touch with his wife. Overall, the mood of *Contempt* is meditative; it is about the impossibility of making a film or sustaining a relationship.

In addition to intellectualizing and de-dramatizing the basic plot, Godard goes so far as to criticize his producers and the type of film they stand for. The character of Prokosch, villain of the film, is a conscious attack on Ponti and Levine. Anti-intellectual, assertive, and self-satisfied to the point of caricature, Prokosch becomes the image of American cultural imperialism as he forces others to bend to his will. He often quotes inane maxims from a tiny book, thus conflating American naiveté with the ideological aggression of Mao's "Little Red Book." Prokosch is specifically linked to Levine when, within the film, a character announces "Jerry, Joe Levine is calling at one from New York." Prokosch is thus Levine's associate, his representative, his other half. Godard also satirizes his producers by showing a few crude and reductive scenes from Prokosch's version of *The Odyssey*.[7] Both Levine and Ponti had produced crude adventure films based on Greek and Roman subjects in the late 1950s and early 1960s; Ponti was the producer of *Ulysses* (1955).

Another unusual aspect of Godard's approach to an "international" film is that he did not simply shoot in English, the language of the multi-national (Hollywood) film corporations. Instead, each character speaks in his or her native language (English, French, German, Italian) and Prokosch's assistant Francesca (Georgia Moll) interprets as necessary. As well as being realistic, this device brings out the film's themes of miscommunication and differing world views. Prokosch's problem in communicating suggests metaphorically that he lives and thinks differently from the other characters. The use of multiple languages also makes *Contempt* easy to subtitle but difficult to dub, as *Variety*'s reviewer astutely noted.[8] In a dubbed version, Francesca's task of repeating what everyone says becomes ludicrous. Perhaps Godard had this consciously in mind, and put in the interpreter as a way to maintain his control against dubbing the film.

Godard's approach to the film transforms a commercial enterprise into a personal as well as philosophical artwork. *Contempt* is a "personal" film in two senses: first, it has certain stylistic and narrative features associated with Godard (elliptical editing, odd combinations of image and sound, numerous citations from other artworks); second, it reflects on Godard's attitudes towards filmmaking and towards this specific film. The setting of international film production, a staple of escapist fiction and film, becomes here an opportunity for the filmmaker's self-doubt. Godard critiques not only Prokosch, but also Paul Javal and even Fritz Lang. Both Javal and Lang are to some extent versions of Godard—filmmakers working on a project they do not respect. The parallels between Javal and Godard are obvious—the relative inexperience in film production, the cultural background, the admiration for American film mixed with a desire to make films differently. Brigitte Bardot even puts on a black wig during a long argument with Javal, which makes her look like Anna Karina, Godard's wife in 1963. Lang's role, for Godard, was "sad" and "touching," because Lang tried to be independent of Prokosch and yet he had followed the wishes of Hollywood producers except at the beginning of his career.[9] This can be read as a projection of Godard's own situation during the filming of *Contempt*—independent and yet not independent of his producers.

One could conclude from the various strategies detailed above that Godard had successfully outfoxed his producers. However, a film does not end with the director's cut. It must be promoted and sold and sometimes altered for distribution, and here producers and distributors take charge.

Carlo Ponti and Joseph Levine had given Godard a free hand during the shooting of *Contempt*, but they were not pleased with the result. Levine's first action was to withhold the film from the 1963 Venice Film Festival. Levine then threatened to recut the film; Godard protested, and decried Levine's lack of understanding. Levine and Godard were, indeed, enormously different in their approaches to film, Godard intensely intellectual and artistic, Levine a great salesman and promoter with no intellectual pretensions. Godard explained to Herbert Feinstein:

> When I was discussing *Le Mépris* with Joseph Levine, I learned little by little that the words did not mean the same things to him that they did to me—He is not a bad man, but I am not either. When we say "picture," it doesn't mean the same thing at all.[10]

Levine and Ponti eventually split on how to revise Godard's cut of *Contempt*. Levine requested additional nude scenes with Bardot to make the film more commercial, and Godard found a way to do this without damaging his film. He shot, in France, an opening scene for the film with Camille nude on her stomach in bed, asking Paul which parts of her body he loves most. This is not a conventional love scene; Bardot's body is treated rather formally, with changes in lighting and filters. The scene is intimate but not erotic, an abstract representation of the love of Camille and Paul. Godard responded very literally to his producers' complaint "Well, you haven't got enough ass in it,"[11] while actually enhancing the thematic and stylistic qualities of *Contempt*.

Carlo Ponti took more extreme measures to reshape *Contempt* to meet his own needs. He dubbed, shortened, and in other ways drastically changed the film. The dubbing destroyed the character of Francesca (she became an interpreter with nothing to interpret) and the film's theme of miscommunication. Ponti's cut eliminated most of the *Odyssey* scenes, so the relationship between Homer's epic and the modern story was lost. The Italian version of the film centers on the romantic triangle of Paul, Camille, and Prokosch. Ponti even removed Georges Delerue's melancholy, almost tragic, score, which in Godard's version of the film is the one element which approximates the grandeur of *The Odyssey*. A jazzy score by Piero Piccioni was substituted.[12]

Contempt was ultimately distributed in three different versions in the home territories of the three producers. It was 100 minutes long in France, 103 minutes long in the United States, 84 minutes long in Italy. The French and the American (subtitled) versions of the film are almost identical; the opening scene requested by Joe Levine is in both. The Italian version, on the other hand, is so different from other versions of *Contempt* that Godard removed his name from Italian prints of the film. Italian critic Adriano Aprà wrote that "The Italian copy of *Il disprezzo* by Godard represents perhaps the most sensational case of betrayal of the original film in the history of film."[13]

To put the dispute between Godard and his producers in a broader perspective, one must remember that art-film directors were newly prominent in the early 1960s, and no one knew what could be expected from the first English-language projects of a Truffaut (*Fahrenheit 451*) or a Polanski (*Repulsion*). In this context, Ponti thought he was getting a big-budget entertainment film starring Brigitte Bardot. Godard, instead, provided a wide-ranging critique of Hollywood producers and Cinecittà-style entertainment films. Godard, Ponti, and Levine learned only "little by little" that they were not working within a common framework. So, *Contempt* is an excellent film based on a misunderstanding.

Godard's retrospective comment on *Contempt* was that it is very important to be one's own producer.[14] After *Contempt*, Godard returned to smaller budgets and to more control over his films. He did not, however, entirely escape the influence of the large American film companies. *Band of Outsiders* and *A Married Woman*, his next two feature films, were largely financed by distribution advances from Columbia Pictures.[15]

Contempt/Le Mépris/Il disprezzo was a commercial success only in France, where the combination of Godard, Bardot, and a strongly positive critical response gave the film a good commercial career (more than 200,000 viewers in first-run Paris theaters). In the United States, the film was held back from a New York opening for several months by censorship. The New York State Board of Regents, a censoring body of the time, refused a license to the film unless cuts were made in some of the nude scenes. Joseph Levine fought this censorship in court and eventually won. Levine was consistent in his quest for a more sensational film: he first fought the director for more nudity and then fought the censor to get approval for the nudity. At any rate, the "uncut" *Contempt* did not attract a substantial American audience, despite a favorable review from *Playboy* (featured in the ad campaign of the film). *Contempt* played for four weeks at the Lincoln Art Theater in New York at the same time that other film imports, notably *Umbrellas of Cherbourg* and *Marriage Italian Style*, were enjoying long runs.

Curiously, the story of the struggle for control of the images and sounds of *Contempt* does not end with the film's theatrical release. The new technology of videotape has made *Contempt*, as well as thousands of other films, available for home viewing. But *Contempt* is available on videotape in the United States in two versions, subtitled and dubbed. The subtitled version presents Godard's cut of the film, with each character speaking his or her own language. The widescreen ratio is lost, replaced by television's 1.33 to 1, but most of the film's subtleties remain. The dubbed version, however, reduces the film to a group of spectacular elements: Brigitte Bardot, Jack Palance, Fritz Lang, and some beautiful cinematography. Palance and Lang's English-language performances remain, but the coherence of Bardot's dialogue is destroyed and she becomes a body, not an actress. The character of Francesca makes no sense, and the complex relationship to *The Odyssey* (which involves mainly the French-speaking characters) is lost. The dubbed videotape gives some idea of what the producers were looking for—a melodrama of adultery with international stars—although it is too fragmented to be a successful melodrama.

Contempt is more successful as a film of art than as a film of commerce/entertainment. Yet clearly both concepts of cinema have shaped, and continue to shape, this film. The interaction of film art versus film commerce/entertainment takes place on at least three interrelated levels: the production process, the film text itself, and the distribution history of the film. *Contempt* thus continues to be, long after its original release, a battleground for different concepts of cinema.

Museum of Modern Art/Film Stills Archive.

7. *Blow-Up,* Swinging London, and the Film Generation

Blow-Up, like *Contempt,* can be approached from the dual perspectives of art and commerce. It is certainly a key work in the distinguished artistic career of Michelangelo Antonioni, one of the world's great film directors. *Blow-Up* has excellent credentials as an art film: script and direction by Antonioni, based on a story by the Argentine modernist Julio Cortázar, and with an emphasis on theme and visual imagery rather than on genres or stars. Yet *Blow-Up* must also be considered an entry into the world of big-budget commercial filmmaking: produced by Carlo Ponti for MGM, made in London at a time when that city was exporting popular culture around the world.

The artistic aspects of *Blow-Up* have monopolized critical discussion. Article after article has delved into the film's ambiguities. The film seems to be particularly attractive to American critics, perhaps because it is one of the few widely admired art films to have achieved extensive distribution in the United States. Without denying the interest of *Blow-Up* criticism, I will concentrate in this essay on the film's social and cultural backdrop. I believe that social and cultural factors can illuminate the film's distinctive look and feel, and can solve some, though not all, of its mysteries. *Blow-Up,* like other Euro-American art films, can be understood as a response to a particular period and to particular film-industry conditions.

The film *Blow-Up* was based not only on Cortázar's short story "Las babas del diablo" (the English translation was titled "Blow-Up" after the success of the film), but also on the article "The Modelmakers," written by Francis Wyndham for the *London Sunday Times Magazine.*[1] Wyndham's article is a long interview with three successful young photographers—Brian Duffy, Terence Donovan, and David Bailey—which describes the milieu of British fashion photography circa 1964. A handful of fashion photographers, with David Bailey perhaps the best-known, were among the new celebrities of London in the 1960s. Young, wealthy, creative, impatient with tradition (most came from working-class backgrounds), they cut dashing figures in the era of the Beatles. Their professional and personal innovations included a more directly sexual approach to fashion, a breakdown of the gap between fashion photography and art photography, and a similar coming together of documentation of an event and creation of an event. The photographers observed the London scene but also helped to create it.

As Alexander Walker notes, the idea of a feature film about the life of a fashion photographer set in London, and based in part on Wyndham's article, did not originate with Antonioni. The highly commercial Italian producer Carlo Ponti, working on a multi-picture production deal with MGM, began discussions on such a film in 1964. At one time David Bailey himself was scheduled to direct the film. However, Bailey turned to other projects, and the "photographer film" was stalled until Antonioni and Ponti came to an agreement on it.[2]

Although Antonioni was not involved in the earliest stages of the "photographer film," he did have ample opportunity to shape it to his own artistic needs. Antonioni conducted extensive research on the lives of London's young fashion photographers, using Francis Wyndham as a consultant. Antonioni and Tonino Guerra, his longtime script collaborator, wrote a screenplay which made the "photographer film" a loose adaptation of the Cortázar story (which concerns a photographer, a mystery, and a crucial scene of making enlargements; it is otherwise quite unlike *Blow-Up*).[3] Antonioni also cast the picture, directed it, and supervised the editing.

The plot of *Blow-Up* presents twenty-four hours in the life of a successful young photographer (David Hemmings). We first see him leaving a flophouse where he has spent the night taking pictures for a book. He jumps into a Rolls-Royce convertible and goes to his studio/ living space for photo sessions with the glamorous Verushka (a celebrity model of the time, who plays herself) and with a group of bizarrely dressed fashion models. Then he leaves to scout an antique store for possible purchases. He visits a park across from the antique store and films a tryst between a young woman (Vanessa Redgrave) and an older man. The woman is disturbed about being filmed, but the Hemmings character says photography is his job. After lunch with his agent Ron, the photographer returns to his studio to develop the pictures from the park. The young woman from the park appears and asks for the film. She eventually leaves with a roll of film (not the right one). The photographer starts developing and enlarging the park photographs and finds in a stand of trees what appears to be a gun pointed at the lovers. In another enlargement he discovers what appears to be a body. He is interrupted by a visit of two miniskirted young girls asking to have their picture taken. He ends up undressing both girls in a sprawl of photo backdrop paper (and presumably having sex with them).

Waking up from this "orgy," the photographer visits the park at night and sees the body. He returns home and finds his studio has been burglarized. The negatives and most of the prints from the park are gone. When he goes next door to talk to his neighbors, a painter and his girlfriend (wife?), they are making love. The photographer then drives to meet his agent at a party. On the way, he thinks he sees the Vanessa Redgrave character; looking for her, he finds himself in a rock club, but she has disappeared. He arrives at the party, but Ron, the agent, is not interested in his story. Ron passes the photographer some marijuana joints, and both men evidently spend the evening getting high. In the morning, the photographer revisits the park; the body is gone. Leaving the park, he encounters some mimes playing a tennis game. At their gestured request, he returns an imaginary tennis ball (invisible, though not inaudible) to the players. The photographer then disappears in mid-frame.

Why was Antonioni interested in a such a "trendy" subject? Without undue psychologizing, a few answers are possible. First, Antonioni had observed the London art and fashion scene in 1964, when he accompanied Monica Vitti to England for the filming of *Modesty Blaise*. At that time he saw something in mod London that intrigued him. In doing interviews about *Blow-Up*, Antonioni several times expressed interest and even a qualified support for the freedom and iconoclasm of mod London. Second, despite his critical reputation, Antonioni had not at this time established himself as a commercial filmmaker. A proud man, he insisted on being treated as a major artist. In a notorious interview with Rex Reed in the *New York Times* (which Antonioni later complained about in a letter to the *Times*), Antonioni expressed resentment about being underpaid and under-recognized in comparison to star actors and to other directors.[4] He may have turned to the fashionable subject of *Blow-Up* in a conscious attempt to make his mark in commercial filmmaking. The success of *Blow-Up* did, in fact, have this result. Antonioni reached a broader public with *Blow-Up* than ever before or since in his career, and the film's success led to a contract for three more English-language films with MGM (only two were ever made: *Zabriskie Point* and *The Passenger*).

Many critics have noted that *Blow-Up* is strikingly different in visual style from Antonioni's earlier films. *Blow-Up* is more colorful, more rapid, more active than the gray-toned, languidly paced Italian films Antonioni made in the early 1960s. The change of style and mood can be attributed to both commercial and artistic attributes of *Blow-Up*. Commercially, *Blow-Up* is a film of "swinging London," of a free and creative youth culture which reached a worldwide audience in the mid-sixties. Academic critics may easily overlook the extent to which the subculture presented in *Blow-Up*—fashion, rock music, pot parties—was in itself attractive to audiences of the time. The film is a detailed look at the successful artists of the British "youth culture," and may have positive connotations independent of Antonioni's personal interpretation of the London scene. MGM's press releases on *Blow-Up* heavily emphasize the youth appeal of modern London, "where teenage pop singing groups have their records sold in shops owned by people their own age, and photographers who have barely started showing drive Rolls-Royces with radio-telephones."[5] Even incidental details of the film may have a powerful attraction; for example, a former student tells me that *Blow-Up* is an important record of sixties rock and roll because it is "the only film with Jimmy Page and Jeff Beck playing together" (in the brief scene of the Yardbirds at the rock club).

Blow-Up can be enjoyed for its beautiful surfaces: the photographer's airy, modern studio; the modeling session with the statuesque Verushka; the quiet neighborhood park; the rock club, and so on. But the attractive visuals of swinging London are only one part of a complex artistic construction. For Antonioni, swinging London represents at least a possible way out of the social world in crisis he had analyzed in his Italian films. In the tetralogy of *L'Avventura* to *Red Desert*, Antonioni had shown a fragmented, confused, anomic society where intimate relationships in particular had lost their meaning. Antonioni told interviewers in the early 1960s that his films portrayed a situation where concepts of love and morality were profoundly out of touch with the actual conditions of life.[6] *Blow-Up* brings a new freedom to these problems. The photographer, with his aesthetic sensibility and his willingness to act on impulse, seems to be less conflicted and less blocked than the protagonists of *L'Avventura* or *La notte*. Casual, sexually available, and open to experience, he suggests a breakout from conformism, a new morality. He is also an artist in a society that values the artistic (note the Rolls-Royce). The visually exciting environment of *Blow-Up* expresses the new possibilities of the character and his milieu.

Blow-Up also, however, contains a critique of this character and of the 1960s youth culture he represents. In the course of the film the photographer's new morality turns out to be severely limited. The photographer lives in an environment where things are often not what they seem, and where no one standard of values prevails. Indeed, as Andrew Tudor has pointed out, reality itself is mutable: a love scene becomes a murder because of a changed "vantage point."[7] In this situation, how does one follow through on a personally and socially meaningful action? The photographer fails to do this, allowing himself to be distracted from reporting the murder. He is ultimately a weak character, limited to the aestheticism and hedonism of his profession and his subculture. The bright colors and rapid movements of *Blow-Up* might thus be seen as distractions and illusions rather than as unambiguous representations of an attractve, mod London.

Another cultural context influencing the production and reception of *Blow-Up* was the evolution of motion picture censorship in the 1960s. The restrictive Motion Picture Production Code governing Hollywood films was rapidly eroding in this period. Many foreign-made films were being successfully released in the United States without a Code seal of approval. In response to this competition, the Code was reorganized and simplified in 1966, with many specific prohibitions eliminated. As part of the reorganization, the category "Suggested for Mature Audiences" (SMA) was added to accommodate films on the margin of the new Code's limits.

A key argument in the censorship debates of the mid-1960s was that rigid censorship codes unduly restricted the possibilities of film art. *Blow-Up* was very much in the middle of this debate, since it was made by an internationally prestigious director; it contained sexually explicit scenes that had not, to this point, been acceptable in a film released by a major Hollywood company; and it was produced by MGM, which had traditionally been one of the Code's staunchest supporters. *Blow-Up* was submitted to the Production Code Administration in 1966, and a deal was worked out with MGM as to what cuts would be needed to qualify for a Code seal with the SMA proviso. The cuts involved two scenes: the photographer's erotic tussling with the teenaged girls, and the lovemaking between the painter and his girlfriend as witnessed by the photographer. However, Antonioni refused to make any changes, saying that he had a contractual right to final cut. MGM backed Antonioni, with a company official commenting that *Blow-Up* was "an artistic masterpiece, which could only be flawed by cutting even such brief deletions as requested by the Code office."[8] *Blow-Up* was ultimately released without a Code seal by "Premier Films" (a subsidiary company of MGM) and under the heading "Carlo Ponti Presents." This was done to avoid putting MGM in explicit conflict with the Production Code, which all the major studios ostensibly supported. MGM thus resorted to a subterfuge in order to release a film which in its explicit sexuality was more akin to the art film than to traditional studio product.

A curious sidelight to this censorship controversy is that MGM actually did cut the film, and a Code-approved SMA label was still being negotiated one month after the film's release in December, 1966. MGM cut a few seconds of the lovemaking between the painter and his girlfriend to tone down the implication that the girlfriend (Sarah Miles) gets excited by having the photographer watch. But MGM made the cut quietly, without a public statement; a *Variety* article suggests that this was done to avoid unfavorable publicity for censoring a filmmaker's work.[9] With the one cut plus *Blow-Up's* strong commercial opening, MGM asked for a reconsideration of the Code seal decision. The Production Code Administration agreed to reconsider, but MGM quickly withdrew its request.[10] Since *Blow-Up* was doing so well without a Code seal, there was no reason for MGM to continue negotiations with the PCA. The Production Code was fast becoming irrelevant. It was replaced by a ratings system in 1968.

The censorship controversy surrounding *Blow-Up* created a great deal of free publicity and thereby contributed to the film's commercial success. *Blow-Up* grossed about $7,000,000 in its 1966–1967 American release, an excellent figure for an art film.[11] It was equally controversial and successful in Italy, where a nationwide ban on the film was quickly overturned. As in the United States, the Italian censorship battle highlighted weaknesses in the existing censorship mechanism and generated enormous interest in the film.[12]

Although there is much merit in the argument that censorship of sexually explicit material restricts film's artistic possibilities, it is important to note that film art and sex in cinema are linked for commercial reasons as well. Historically, the popularity of the foreign film in the United States after World War II—and continuing to the present—can be explained at least in part by the frank attitudes toward sexuality presented by the European imports. This does not mean that foreign films are necessarily calculating and exploitative in their use of sexuality. In *Blow-Up*, the sexually provocative material is integral to the milieu being studied, and to Antonioni's thematic concerns. But viewer interpretation can separate and emphasize the sexual display, making *Blow-Up* an arty backdrop for several sexually daring scenes. This possible "reading" undoubtedly was a factor in the film's box office success.

A third social and cultural context of *Blow-Up* was the motion picture audience of the 1960s. Antonioni's broadening of interests beyond the ennui of the Italian upper-middle class came at a moment when film audiences were unusually open to artistic and philosophical dimensions of motion pictures. The mid-1960s was the era of the "Film Generation." Stanley Kauffmann used this phrase in a 1966 essay to describe "the first generation that has matured in a culture in which the film has been of accepted serious relevance, however that seriousness may be defined." According to Kauffmann, "Even its [the Film Generation's] appreciations of sheer entertainment films reflect this overall serious view." Kauffmann and others have described the 1960s as the period in which film replaced the novel as the preeminent cultural form in the United States and Europe.[13]

In this situation, audiences were willing to accept *Blow-Up* as both popular entertainment and philosophical exploration. Audiences and critics enjoyed playing the game of what the film might mean. In some cases, *Blow-Up*'s meaning and value were heatedly debated in the popular press. In Baltimore, Anne Childress of the *News-American* described *Blow-Up* as "the best movie I have ever seen," but Andrea Herman of the same paper responded by labeling the film "a weary senseless sequence of events that never add up to anything artistically or otherwise."[14] Pauline Kael's negative review of the film in the *New Republic* was met by a salvo of complaints from angry readers.[15] In *Playboy*, Antonioni was accorded not only a review, but a lengthy and serious "Playboy Interview" as well.[16] And *Blow-Up* criticism appeared in any number of literary and philosophical journals. It is difficult to imagine any film of the early 1990s being so hotly debated in both popular and specialized publications.

Charles Eidsvik suggests that *Blow-Up*'s audience appeal depends on Antonioni's respect for the "hypothesizing and perceptual processes" of narrative cinema. Antonioni engages the viewer with two fascinating puzzles: first, the identity of a protagonist who shifts roles frequently; and second, the nature and consequences of the murder revealed by the protagonist's enlargements. With the viewer "seduced" (Eidsvik's term) by these two rather traditional puzzles, which would not be out of place in a Hitchcock film, Antonioni's film proceeds to more unsettling developments. It shows that perception, understanding, and action depend on numerous subjective and social elements; there is no one clear path for the photographer to take in responding to the murder. The film concludes with the thoroughly enigmatic scene of the imaginary tennis ball. At this point the viewer is still trying to "solve" the narrative puzzle; since the puzzle is unsolvable, the spectator has been transported from a traditional to a modernist film-viewing experience.[17]

I would add two historical-cultural factors to Eidsvik's formalist account of *Blow-Up*'s appeal. First, the film's "difficult" themes of ambiguous perception and multiple levels of reality were familiar to audiences of the time. *Blow-Up* was made in the period when pop culture figures such as Timothy Leary, Carlos Castaneda, and innumerable rock stars were playing with levels of perception and reality in relation to the use of psychedelic drugs. In *Blow-Up*, the pot party is a negative moment which blocks the photographer from taking action about the murder. However, the viewer can choose to avoid Antonioni's moralism (which, itself, is presented in an ambiguous context) and to concentrate on the film's mutable surfaces. This reading of the film brings it close to the perceptual play of the drug-influenced pop culture of the 1960s.

A second factor to emphasize is that only the serious audience described by Kauffmann, an audience willing to look beneath the surface of a film narrative, would have followed *Blow-Up*'s trajectory from conventional to philosophical mysteries. As Kauffmann's article states, film and audience are interdependent.[18] The imaginative and challenging narrative strategy described by Eidsvik requires a serious and receptive audience. Conversely, the Film Generation audience needs films like *Blow-Up*. Without this symbiotic relationship between art film and film audience in the 1960s, *Blow-Up* would have been an inaccessible, elitist film.

The point to be made is not that a film can be reduced to a few historical and social conditions. But I do object to criticism that looks at *Blow-Up* as the timeless masterpiece of the great filmmaker Antonioni adapting the great writer Cortázar. Instead, *Blow-Up* is the point of convergence of a number of important trends. It is Antonioni, Ponti, and MGM's foray into the youth culture of swinging London. It is carefully balanced between the prestige of the art film and the commercial appeals of fashion, sex, and rock and roll. It is a conservative Hollywood studio's experiment with an English-language art film and with sexually explicit scenes. In its mix of youth culture and philosophy it is specifically aimed at the audience Kauffmann dubbed the "Film Generation." The extraordinary achievement of *Blow-Up* lies in its rich synthesis of Europe and Hollywood, sex and philosophy, art and entertainment.

8. Pasolini's *The Canterbury Tales:* The Estrangement of an English Classic

The Canterbury Tales was one of the last films made by the poet-novelist-essayist-filmmaker Pier Paolo Pasolini, who died in 1975. Through the 1960s, Pasolini had been a writer-director of iconoclastic and sometimes hermetic feature films based on both original scripts (e.g., *Teorema*, 1968) and classic texts (e.g., *Oedipus Rex*, 1967). In the early 1970s, however, Pasolini's filmmaking underwent a dramatic shift. He began to make populist films for a broad international audience, based on well-known story compilations of the Middle Ages. Pasolini announced this project as the "Trilogy of Life," consisting of *The Decameron* (1971), *The Canterbury Tales* (1972), and *The Arabian Nights* (1974). He described it as "a sort of popular, liberated and erotic trilogy, very sympathetic to humanity, with a great deal of love for man and his nature."[1] The films of the trilogy were not explicitly political or didactic, but they did present pre-capitalist and pre-bourgeois societies characterized (according to Pasolini) by simpler and more positive relationships between humanity and physical reality, including the reality of human sexuality. Thus, these alternate pasts contained a criticism of the consumerist and alienated present.

Pasolini's statements about the trilogy portray it as entirely the product of his own artistic development in face of contemporary events. However, these three films must also be situated within film industry practice, since even auteur films require complex business arrangements and a budget of hundreds of thousands, if not millions, of dollars. The films of the Pasolini trilogy were made possible by the support of producer Alberto Grimaldi. They are part of a distinguished group of films produced by Grimaldi in the late 1960s and the 1970s, with majority financing by the American company United Artists. Other important films in the group are *Fellini Satyricon* (1969), Gillo Pontecorvo's *Burn* (1970), Bernardo Bertolucci's *Last Tango in Paris* (1972), and a few years later Bertolucci's *1900* (1976) and *Fellini Casanova* (1976). Hank Werba of *Variety* described Grimaldi's early 1970s films as "projects of global resonance."[2]

The Grimaldi films are clearly socially critical films as well as spectacles, with a leftist political orientation and, in several films, an emphasis on sexuality as both symptom and catalyst of social change. The two films most similar to the Pasolini trilogy are *Fellini Satyricon* and *Last Tango in Paris. Satyricon,* with its emphasis on sexuality and its metaphor of the decadent past as an image of the disordered present, is probably a model for the Pasolini trilogy. This is not to say that Fellini and Pasolini have similar viewpoints on the past. Fellini seems to reject the decadence of the past while at the same time glorying in it. Pasolini, more consistent, presents a kind of radical innocence in the past which can serve as an image of sexual liberation in the present. *Last Tango in Paris* is a film about sexuality as a personal and social catalyst. The meetings between Marlon Brando and Maria Schneider in an almost-empty apartment bring into question the events and values of their "other" lives. Pasolini does something similar in the Trilogy of Life, but by presenting whole alternate societies rather than concentrating on the couple.

Before proceeding, we might question whether *The Canterbury Tales* should be considered a Euro-American film at all. As with many Italian films, the issue of the film's primary language needs to be resolved. *The Canterbury Tales* was shot mainly in England, but without live sound. English-dubbed and Italian-dubbed versions were then prepared. Which should be considered the original or preferred version? For some films (e.g., *Fellini Satyricon* or *Fellini Casanova*) this question is impossible to answer. However, in the case of *The Canterbury Tales* Pasolini's comments at the Berlin Film Festival in 1972 suggest that the English-language version of the film should be taken as primary. Pasolini talked in Berlin about an English soundtrack carefully prepared to present not the "English of the Old Vic," but the "English spoken on all the levels of society." He described the Italian soundtrack as "an attempt to find the equivalent of the English version." And he said that he was waiting for a completed English version to decide if he liked *The Canterbury Tales* better than *The Decameron.*[3]

A few years earlier, Pasolini had told Oswald Stack that he actually preferred dubbed soundtracks to live sound, because dubbing "enriches a character" and gives the filmmaker more ability to intervene.[4] In *The Canterbury Tales,* for example, the English soundtrack includes a number of working-class and rural dialects from England and Scotland. This mixing of dialects is an example of directorial intervention on the soundtrack. I believe Pasolini wanted a mix of dialects for two reasons: first, to insist on a worker-peasant orientation to the story; and second, to avoid an overly naturalistic "placement" of the tales in either a contemporary or a historical reality.

Pasolini's adaptation of Chaucer is a loose one. Only seven of Chaucer's tales and two prologues are included in the film, and this includes one instance (The Cook's Tale) where Pasolini has taken off from a brief fragment to invent an original tale of his own. Pasolini has also been highly selective in his choice of tales. He prefers the most popular tales, the rough jests of the lower classes rather than the refinements of aristocrats. In the terms of fourteenth-century England, Pasolini emphasizes the world of the "churls" and excludes the world of the "gentles." Pasolini's England is therefore materialist, sensual, and pragmatic, though not without its supernatural beings.

Pasolini has eliminated most of Chaucer's elaborate structure of prologues and multiple narrators. The film does begin with a scene of the pilgrims at the Inn at Southwark, but this scene mainly serves to visually situate the story in the Middle Ages. After a brief statement from the innkeeper that he will guide the pilgrims and require each one to tell a tale, we see nothing more of the pilgrims until a very brief scene of the arrival at Canterbury. Some of the tales are juxtaposed without transitions. In other cases, Pasolini breaks the flow of the tales to show himself as Geoffrey Chaucer doing the actual writing. So instead of using the pilgrims as intermediaries between the writer/filmmaker and the reader/viewer, Pasolini presents a more direct relationship between the teller and the tale.

There are two sorts of tale in Pasolini's film—the tale of erotic exchange and the tale of death and damnation.[5] In the erotic tales an authority figure is cuckolded by a younger, more attractive man. In the Merchant's Tale, for example, the allegorically named January marries the young and beautiful May, who takes advantage of her aging husband's blindness to make love with the young Damiano. In the tales of death the repressive institution of the Church and/or the characters' own weaknesses lead to death and damnation. For example, in the Friar's Tale, a summoner (the agent of an ecclesiastical court) befriends a devil, agreeing that both engage in similar work. Then the devil claims the summoner's soul and dispatches him to Hell.

In general, the erotic tales dominate the first half of the film, the tales of death the second half (Pasolini's order of tales is quite different from Chaucer's). The first half thus moves toward a freer sexuality, the second half toward death and dissolution. However, the Friar's Tale is the second tale presented. This counters the celebratory mood of much of the film's first part, and brings into question Pasolini's notion of the "Trilogy of Life" as sympathetic and full of love for man. The Friar's Tale and the three tales which close Pasolini's *Canterbury Tales* expose human cruelty and weakness as well as the omnipresence of death. Instead of a celebration of life, this film can be seen as a struggle between two

THE CANTERBURY TALES
The Miller's Tale and (below) *Pier Paolo Pasolini as Chaucer.*

opposed visions—the joys of the erotic and the sensual versus the terrors of cruelty, repression, and death. *The Canterbury Tales* is certainly the darkest in tone of the films of the Trilogy.

An original and fascinating aspect of Pasolini's adaptation is his approach to presenting the Middle Ages in images and sounds. The director and his crew shot almost the entire film in the towns and countryside of England,[6] using authentic-looking locations in Bath, Canterbury, Wells, etc. to suggest a medieval atmosphere. The physical environment of the film—costumes, landscapes, public spaces—is convincingly different from modern England, although it may not be period accurate in detail. Several scenes include wide-angle, deep-focus shots which establish the "otherness" of the environment. Pasolini also uses a number of English and Scottish non-actors of modest social background (along with a few professional actors) to play the primarily lower-class characters of his film. Their faces create a worker-peasant context which could not be duplicated by a cast of professional actors.

These techniques have led one critic to call *The Canterbury Tales* a neorealist film of the Middle Ages.[7] Neorealist elements are certainly present. However, the film also has some extremely calculated non-realist elements. For example, it departs from realism by having Pasolini himself play Chaucer (thus introducing reflexivity), by the presence of Pasolini regulars Franco Citti and Ninetto Davoli in key roles, by an extended homage to Chaplin in the Cook's Tale, and by the heterogeneity of the dialects on the soundtrack. What Pasolini has done is to break with the realist conventions of presenting the past on film. He is in some instances *more realistic* than the accepted conventions (e.g., in shooting on location in the English countryside), in some instances *less realistic* (e.g., in the reflexive moments and the dubbing). The overall effect is that the mode of presenting the past can no longer be taken for granted. Pasolini departs from the British and American naturalistic approach of presenting a past which seems to be factual and unmanipulated, and which downplays its own conventions, contradictions, and anachronisms. This is the approach used by everything from Olivier's Shakespeare adaptations to British epics to Warner Bros. biography films. Pasolini's alternative approach is to present a past which mixes austere realism and personal notations. The past in Pasolini's film becomes a wondrous and unpredictable country.

The estrangement ("making strange") of the past in *The Canterbury Tales* has an important political dimension. For most of the twentieth century the United States and Great Britain have dominated the world's mass media and have therefore shaped the perception of the past, of other nations, etc. Many regions of the world have been distorted and stereotyped in popular media following Anglo-American points of view. Pasolini's film reverses this media hegemony. It presents Chaucerian England as a strange, exotic land seen from an "Italianized" point of view—using neorealist techniques, Pasolini's role as Chaucer, and various authorial asides to create this perspective. Even the mixture of dialects evokes an Italian viewpoint, since Italy has traditionally been a country of many dialects and no strong national language.[8] Chaucer's England is seen as poor, primitive, and oppressed by organized religion, yet also joyous, direct, in touch with feelings and with sexuality. In other words, medieval England becomes something like Pasolini's vision of a pre-bourgeois, pre-consumerist world which his other films locate in the past (*The Decameron*) or in the Italian slums of the present (*Accatone*).

In his statements about *The Canterbury Tales* Pasolini did not emphasize the film's critique of England and of dominant Anglo-Saxon culture. He described his film in simple terms: "an Italian read Chaucer and at night he dreamed of what he had read."[9] No political critique here. But by making England a poor, primitive place where fairies and devils walk abroad, Pasolini contests the dominant image of England as rich, powerful, rational, and modern. This strategy is consistent with Pasolini's love of poor peasant cultures and hatred of advanced capitalist societies. Pasolini, in some ways a disciple of Antonio Gramsci, is (in both Italian and world contexts) for the primitive South and against the industrialized North.

Glimpses of this same attitude can be seen in other Pasolini films. For example, Pasolini has taken *The Decameron*, a work by the Tuscan Giovanni Boccaccio, and set it in the slums of Naples (emblematic of southern Italy). A key literary work associated with the dominant cultural center of Florence thus becomes, in its film adaptation, a celebration of the passion and spontaneity of less "advanced" Southern Italy. Also, in *The Gospel According to Matthew*, Pasolini has a Roman legion (representing Europe and power) attack a poor Jewish village (the Third World). Since the village being photographed is actually in southern Italy, the North-South split in the film can also be applied to contemporary Italy.

In *The Canterbury Tales*, as in *The Gospel According to Matthew*, the presentation of a peasant culture has both historical and contemporary resonances. Historically, Pasolini suggests that *The Canterbury Tales*, a founding work of English culture, derives much of its appeal from the appearance of the lower classes—who have often been excluded from "serious literature." In contemporary terms, Pasolini's use of lower-class urban and rural non-actors to portray a peasant culture is even more subversive. These smiling men and women with crooked teeth and reddened cheeks suggest that, after two centuries of industrialization, there may still be a trace of pre-capitalist culture in the England of today.

However, Pasolini himself talked about the difficulty of filming in England. He felt less comfortable, less in touch with the pre-capitalist world in England than in Naples (*The Decameron*) or in the Middle East (*The Arabian Nights*). Pasolini complained that the people he worked with lacked a sense of humor and a free and natural approach to sexuality.[10] In other words, the location filming in England did not fit perfectly with Pasolini's preconceived vision. This may be one reason why *The Canterbury Tales* is the darkest and most conflicted film in the Trilogy of Life.

The difficulties of filming in England may also be at the root of some of the film's inconsistencies. Pasolini was not a fluent English speaker. Therefore, the dubbing, while extraordinary in concept, is sometimes lacking in execution. For example, the dying Thomas in the Summoner's Tale who bequeaths a fart to a greedy friar is given a learned voice quite alien to his character. In general, the film's visual images, which evoke the fourteenth century based on paintings of the period, are more impressive than the soundtrack. Also, the tales themselves are of unequal merit. The Friar's Tale, the Pasolini-invented Cook's Tale, and the Reeve's Tale of a miller cuckolded by two students are nicely done. But the Merchant's Tale is hurt by the over-exuberant dialogue of Hugh Griffith (who plays January), and the tale adapted from the Wife of Bath's Prologue is badly edited and silly. Pasolini wastes the possibilities of using the Wife of Bath as a self-conscious and socially critical character.

The Canterbury Tales received an extremely mixed popular and critical reception. The film had a strong theatrical release in Italy, but it failed miserably in Great Britain. In the United States it was held out of release until 1980, when it played in a few art theaters. The critical reception has been just as mixed. Some critics have treated *The Canterbury Tales* and the Trilogy as an important part of the work of a major filmmaker. Giacomo Gambetti, for example, describes *The Canterbury Tales* as "rich in intelligent creative solutions" and ideologically astute.[11] Other critics see the films of the Trilogy as an error, a sellout. Robert Kolker, a distinguished American critic of European films, refers to *The Decameron* and *The Canterbury Tales* as simply "pornography."[12]

In my view, Pasolini's film of *The Canterbury Tales* is not pornographic in terms of theme and approach. The extraordinary vision of the Middle Ages and the thematic emphasis on death as well as eros mark this film as a serious work. In the Wife of Bath's Prologue (Pasolini's version) character psychology is so attenuated as to suggest pornography, but the film's overall narrative design adds the subtlety and depth that may be lacking in individual tales. There is a good deal of nudity in the film. However, this nudity is essential to Pasolini's strategy of presenting a directness of desires and feelings in the past, and thus creating an implicit contrast with an alienated present. Also, nudity in *The Canterbury Tales* does not remain within the strict codes of heterosexual pornography. It features both male and female nudity, and refuses to privilege the male heterosexual gaze.

The question of pornography becomes more complicated when one considers the reception of *The Canterbury Tales*. Pasolini may have created a serious film in which sexuality has a critical and contestatory dimension. Nevertheless, his film was experienced by many as a pornographic movie presenting a wide variety of sexual play. The success of *The Canterbury Tales* in Italy probably had more to do with its sexual explicitness than with its art-film qualities. The explicitness of *The Decameron* and *The Canterbury Tales* was so sensational in an Italian context that the two films were widely imitated. Mira Liehm lists a number of low-budget offspring designed to exploit the notoriety of Pasolini's films: *Decameron Number 2, The Last Decameron, Hot Nights of Decameron, The Other Canterbury Tales, Canterbury Number 2.*[13] In the United States, *The Canterbury Tales* was kept off movie screens precisely because the distributor wanted to avoid being linked to pornography. United Artists distributed the X-rated *Last Tango in Paris* to American theaters, but it evidently did not wish to be associated with the sexual display of *The Canterbury Tales*.

Pasolini himself was very sensitive to the reception of the films of the Trilogy. In 1975, he published an essay entitled "Rejection of the Trilogy of Life," which discusses how the three films had been distorted and co-opted by "consumerist power." According to Pasolini, his films used "'innocent' bodies" and sexuality to revolt against the "unreality" of a present dominated by the mass media. But Pasolini in 1975 no longer believes in the innocence of youthful bodies. He is desperately unhappy about the decay of Italian youth and Italian society in general. The situation is so degraded that the past can no longer function as a critique of the present; the intended critique is "cancelled out" by "a tolerance as vast as it is false." Films intended as calls for personal/sexual liberation are tolerated and enjoyed as pornographic amusements (although the essay never uses the term "pornography"). Pasolini's response was to make a far more shocking and intolerable film: *Salo* (1975), a conflation of De Sade's *The 120 Days of Sodom* and the last days of Italian Fascism.[14]

In the case of *Blow-Up*, controversy about sexually explicit material assisted in the wide dissemination and discussion of a complex and challenging film. In the case of *The Canterbury Tales*, however, sexual explicitness interfered with the film's distribution and reception. The sexual display of *Blow-Up* was legitimized in the United States by the debate on censorship that was ongoing in the 1960s, by Antonioni's reputation as an art-film director, and by the fashionable subject of the London youth culture. *The Canterbury Tales* benefited from no such legitimations. The battle against censorship had largely been won by 1972, Pasolini was an unknown in comparison to Fellini or Antonioni, and the film's medieval setting had no special interest to the American public. Further, *The Canterbury Tales* is disturbing, crude, and at times blasphemous, whereas *Blow-Up* is always very tasteful. The differing fortunes of the two films show that art + sex was not an infallible formula for the success of a Euro-American art film, even in the period 1960–1973.

However, over the last few years Pasolini has been (belatedly) gaining recognition as a filmmaker. A major Pasolini retrospective toured North America in the spring and summer of 1990. *The Canterbury Tales* and a number of other Pasolini films have been released on videotape. An important new book has come out, Naomi Greene's *Pier Paolo Pasolini: Cinema as Heresy*. Pasolini's vision of medieval England may yet escape the label of "pornography" to find an appreciative audience in the United States.

9. *Paris, Texas,* an American Dream

Paris, Texas is a paradoxical film which manages to be thoroughly American and thoroughly European at the same time. On the one hand, this is an English-language road movie set in the American Southwest with script by Sam Shepard and music by guitarist Ry Cooder. It stars Harry Dean Stanton, a veteran character actor who has played in numerous Westerns. The mix is exciting, authentic, and evocative of the American West. On the other hand, *Paris, Texas* is a character-oriented film about the loneliness and angst of a male wanderer. It has substantial links to earlier movies directed by Wim Wenders, and to the existential search for meaning and value in many European films.

Wenders had thrown himself obsessively into American filmmaking during *Hammett,* the film he directed for Francis Coppola's Zoetrope Studios. He lived for six months in a San Francisco apartment where Hammett had also lived, trying, perhaps, to "become" his subject.[1] A German filmmaker visiting Berkeley at this time wrote sarcastic comments about Wenders' attempt to be more American than the Americans.[2] However, Wenders was not comfortable with the Hollywood-style production apparatus of *Hammett,* nor with the rather impersonal film that resulted. So, for *Paris, Texas* he attempted a film that would be recognizably American in setting, European in production methods, and a blend (Euro-American) in theme and style.

Wenders and executive producer Chris Sievernich put together financing for this English-language film from strictly European sources. The production companies of record were Wenders' company, Road Movies (Berlin), and Anatole Dauman's Argos Films (Paris). The film's end credits add acknowledgements for Pro-ject Film (Munich) and the television networks Channel Four (London) and Westdeutscher Rundfunk (Cologne). Don Ranvaud notes that nine different financing sources were ultimately used to arrive at a budget of $2,000,000.[3]

Since the filming of *Paris, Texas* in 1983, the device of securing European funds to support an English-language production has become more common. It allows filmmakers to use European resources (including the subsidy system) while at the same time tailoring a film to the U.S.–dominated international market. However, *Paris, Texas* is unusual in its use of the low-budget, piecemeal financing characteristic of European art films. More recent Euro-American art films have been backed, in major part, by large production companies (e.g., Gaumont in France, Neue Constantin in Germany) eager to break into the world market.

The European art-film financing gave Wenders the trade-off of substantial autonomy in exchange for a tight budget. On *Hammett*, there had been a large budget but also close supervision by executive producer Francis Coppola. For *Paris, Texas*, Wenders worked on location with a small, hand-picked team of collaborators (scriptwriters Sam Shepard and L. M. "Kit" Carson, cinematographer Robbie Muller, assistant director Claire Denis, producers Sievernich and Don Guest). The European backers were far removed from day-to-day production and post-production decisions. *Paris, Texas* was a financial gamble, since the film was made without a guarantee from an American distributor (*Hammett* had a distribution contract from Orion as part of a package of Zoetrope films). However, the modest budget and the support from film and television companies in three European countries minimized the risk. As it happens, the film won the Golden Palm (first prize) at Cannes, and then was bought by Twentieth Century Fox for North American distribution.

Paris, Texas begins with Travis (Harry Dean Stanton) wandering in dusty suit, tie, and baseball cap through the desert of Southwest Texas. He enters a store, sucks on some ice, and collapses. A doctor then calls Travis's brother, Walt (Dean Stockwell), in Los Angeles, for help with this new patient, who will not speak. When Walt arrives in Terlingua, Texas, he finds that Travis has left the doctor's clinic. Walt discovers Travis walking in the desert, and they start back to Los Angeles. They drive back because Travis is unwilling to fly.

Walt and his wife Anne (Aurore Clément) have adopted Travis's son Hunter (Hunter Carson), because both Travis and his wife, Jane, have been missing for four years. Travis's reappearance, and his gradual return to health (talking, eating, sleeping), causes considerable strain in Walt's family. Hunter must learn to accept his "real" father, and Anne and Walt must adjust to sharing, perhaps losing, their son. After a few days, Hunter decides to go with Travis to Houston to look for Jane. This devastates Anne and Walt.

Travis finds Jane (Nastassja Kinski) working at the Keyhole Club, a strange establishment where men pay to look at women and talk to them in fantasy environments. The men talk on the telephone in small, darkened booths; the women can be seen in brightly lit rooms labeled "pool," "hotel," and so on. The women normally cannot see their customers. On his first visit, Travis questions Jane on whether she will go home with customers. She says no; she is not a prostitute. On his second visit, Travis tells Jane the story of their life as a couple, including his pathological jealousy and the pain he caused her (e.g., chaining her to the stove in their trailer). Jane recognizes Travis, and forgives him. But Travis cannot forgive himself. He sends Jane to meet Hunter in a Houston hotel room, and sets off alone in his truck at twilight.

At the simplest level, *Paris, Texas* can be seen as a "visit to America" film, a visual tour of picturesque parts of the West. European directors are particularly fond of those regions of the United States which present distinctive landscapes and cultures: the desert Southwest, the South, California. This film begins with a helicopter shot of the wastelands of far Southwest Texas, establishing the "otherness" of the environment. The camera quickly discovers Travis wandering through the desert landscape. Throughout the film, Travis is linked to the desert as well as to modern industrial wastelands (e.g., freeways). Travis's brother Walt, on the other hand, is associated with the complexities and comforts of modern society (cars, airplanes, a suburban house). Travis's reintroduction to civilization gives Wenders and Robbie Muller the opportunity to create striking images of human society impinging on nature—e.g., the motel sign advertising "TV" rising out of the desert. From Travis's point of view, the motels, stores, and restaurants seen along the freeway are bizarre and confining. From Walt's perspective, such images are normal. By presenting both perspectives in the film's first half hour, Wenders and Muller add a thematic complexity to the Southwest's visual beauty.

Paris, Texas can also be seen as a successful blend of American genres. We start with a lone man wandering in the rugged landscape that is so familiar from hundreds of Western films. This man is not a gunfighter like Shane, but rather a man whose marital problems have left him shattered and mute. He is not about to save the ranchers; instead, he needs saving himself. This aspect of the film began with Sam Shepard's book *Motel Chronicles*, a loose collection of poems and prose fragments, and particularly with the description of a man who burns his suitcase at the side of the road and wanders naked into the desert.[4] Given the emphasis on long car trips from Texas to California and back again, *Paris, Texas* can also be viewed as a road movie. Gaylyn Studlar describes the road movie as "a modern version of the saddle-tramp story which brings together the American car-centered culture as a symbol of freedom and mobility and, therefore, individual liberty, with a validation of living on the periphery of society—often, in a buddy system of male cameraderie."[5] The importance of this usually American genre to Wenders can be seen in the name of his Berlin-based production company—Road Movies Filmproduktion. As *Paris, Texas* progresses, though, the generic situation of brothers on the road changes to focus on family issues. First we see the tensions within Walt's family, then Travis and Hunter set off in search of Jane. The story of the wild and rugged Western wilderness has been transformed into a family melodrama.

Paris, Texas began as a plunge into American cinema, a plunge into "otherness" with reflexive elements omitted. Wenders and Sam Shepard worked on a simple, straightforward script. Wenders and Robbie Muller agreed that there would be no pictorial references in the images, that they would view the landscapes of the American West with fresh eyes. Because of the new script collaborator and the new setting, *Paris, Texas* does develop a directness and emotional power that are new for Wenders. But it does not remain a straightforward drama of the American West. A number of elements including title, casting, and narrative references break the straight-ahead, road-movie pattern.

What are we to make of the title, *Paris, Texas*? Within the film's diegesis, *Paris, Texas* is the place where Travis's parents first made love, the place where he thinks he was conceived. Symbolically, *Paris, Texas* is an impossible space, an oxymoron, since "Paris" and "Texas" are separate entities, separate experiences. According to Travis, his father used to say his mother was from "Paris . . . Texas," with the pause setting up false expectations and suggesting a discord between the couple. Eventually the father began to believe his own jest (that his wife was a fancy woman), and to become jealous of her. This split between the parents is mirrored by the estrangement of Travis and Jane, and even by the problems of Walt and Anne. Travis wants to escape from the separation he now feels, and to return to the "home," at once idealized and impossible, represented by the film's title. His anguish stems in large part from the impossibility of going back.

The title *Paris, Texas* can also be seen as Wenders' reflection on the synthesis of European culture and American culture. In this film he brings Paris to Texas, the Paris of the personal filmmaking of the French New Wave, the Paris of Anatole Dauman's Argos Films, the Paris of his own formative experiences (as a student in Paris, Wenders spent long hours at the Cinémathèque Française). He tries to make an American movie, and also to maintain his identity as a European art-film director. Wenders' ambivalence and tension are well-presented in a long poem/essay entitled "The American Dream," which was published in 1984:

> I've lived for seven years in America.
> What happened to my own American dream?
> And can it be separated from the dream
> that America dreams of itself?
> If it is still dreaming at all.[6]

Clearly, the film *Paris, Texas* is Wenders' "own American dream," and a number of markers separate it "from the dream that America dreams of itself."

Consider, for example, the three European actors who appear in *Paris, Texas*. In the film's first few minutes, Travis is treated by an eccentric German doctor (played by film director Bernhard Wicki) in a clinic at the Texas-Mexico border. Walt's wife, Anne, who works with her husband in Los Angeles, is played by a French actress. And Jane, Travis's wife, whose absence is the focus of much of the film, is played by German actress Nastassya Kinski. The simplest explanation of the use of European actors in an American road movie is that their presence may be necessary to Wenders and Sievernich's European backers, either to meet co-production requirements or to help attract German and French audiences. But their presence may also be Wenders' way of pointing to the paradoxes of having a German filmmaker make a hyper-American movie. The film is not only Travis's attempt to reconcile the opposite poles of "Paris" and "Texas," it is also Wenders' attempt to unite these opposites. Wenders is making an American road movie, but also a fairly typical Wenders movie—European financing, small crew, location shooting, a sensitive but inexpressive hero who can be reached only by another male (*The American Friend, Kings of the Road*) or by a child (*Alice in the Cities*).

If we view *Paris, Texas* as a European director's work, omitting for the moment the contributions of Sam Shepard and others, then the film is representative of many Euro-American art films which view the United States as an alternative, an escape, a new start. Some films find a utopian situation in the United States: *Another Man, Another Chance, Bagdad Cafe*. Other films find a failed utopia: *Alamo Bay, Stroszek, Zabriskie Point*. Still others, like *Model Shop*, are inconclusive. *Paris, Texas* describes neither utopia nor dystopia, but rather a new start in an imperfect world for Travis and, by extension, Wenders. *Paris, Texas* is a breakthrough film for Wenders because the hero is able to feel and to articulate much more effectively than in any of his previous films.[7] Travis and Jane's long conversation at the Keyhole Club involves strong moments of revelation and reconciliation. Possibilities of love and healing open up that were not available to the hip loners of Wenders' *Wrong Movement* or *Kings of the Road.*

An alternate perspective would see the emotional dynamics of *Paris, Texas* as primarily Sam Shepard's work. Shepard's plays typically present emotional and highly verbal confrontations within a family. Often, the plays revolve around deeply hidden family secrets (e.g., *Fool for Love, Buried Child*). The domestic violence in Travis and Jane's marriage fits this Shepard theme. And the long monologues by Travis and Jane at the Keyhole Club were written at the last minute by Shepard and delivered word-for-word by the actors. Wenders and Robbie Muller contributed the haunting visuals of this scene (e.g., reflections which superimpose the faces or place them side by side). But Shepard's monologues set the emotional tone.

Kathe Geist suggests that *Paris, Texas* can be seen as a combination of Shepard's and Wenders' emotional styles. Wenders' characters "tend to deal with each other at one remove—through pictures, notes or by running away . . . Shepard's characters, on the other hand, generally confront each other directly, often violently." "Wendersian devices" such as Travis's tape-recorded goodbye to Hunter mediate the raw power of Shepard's speeches.[8] Geist's discussion provides a key to understanding how *Paris, Texas* can be an American movie and a Wenders movie at the same time. Wenders takes the power and directness of Shepard and adds his own hesitations, his own "emotional coolness."[9] He wants to jump into American filmmaking, but also to retain a distance.

This dialectic between direct and distanced emotion becomes very important in the film's last few scenes. Shepard and Wenders have constructed a situation where the family could be united, since Travis and Jane have confessed to each other and found mutual understanding. At this point in production (the film was shot more or less in sequence), Harry Dean Stanton lobbied for the family to stay together, Shepard wanted Travis and Hunter to continue their travels, and Wenders insisted that Travis should leave Hunter with Jane. Wenders overruled Stanton and Shepard and used his own ending.[10] Wenders explains that during the first visit to the Keyhole Club Travis feels the same destructive jealousy that had wrecked his marriage to Jane. Therefore, he cannot resume family life; he can only bring mother and child together.[11] This ending is impractical and irresponsible in terms of family dynamics, because Travis has taken Hunter away from a stable home with Walt and Anne and given him to a mother who works in a sleazy club. But the ending might make more sense as Wenders' refusal to let go of his own artistic individuality, which in past films has focused on alienation and guilt. Providing a conventional happy ending would bring Wenders into the mainstream of American cinema. Despite his fascination with things American, Wenders refuses the happy ending and sends his character off alone. *Paris, Texas* becomes "my own American dream," the dream of an unreconciled loner.

THE LAST EMPEROR
Richard Vuu as the boy emperor, and (below) John Lone, Joan Chen.

10. *The Last Emperor:* Pleasures and Dangers of the Exotic

The Last Emperor was an Italian-British-Chinese co-production of daunting size and complexity. The producer was Englishman Jeremy Thomas, the director Bernardo Bertolucci. The Beijing Film Studio and China Film Coproduction were the Chinese partners. The film's shooting schedule included sixteen weeks in China and eight weeks in Italy. Postproduction was centered in London. Actors for speaking roles were recruited primarily from the Chinese populations of large American cities, because American-accented English was preferred. However, some actors were found in China, Great Britain, and Hong Kong. Financing was originally provided by a consortium of five banks. Hill, Samuel of London was the lead bank, and other members of the consortium came from Great Britain, the Netherlands, Sweden, and Austria. The bank loans were gradually offset by pre-sales to distributors in Europe, Japan, and North America. Hemdale, a British company, bought North American rights to the film for "a little less than half" of the production budget of $25,000,000.[1] These rights were eventually sold to Columbia Pictures.

American financial participation in the film was consciously limited by the producer and director. Bertolucci, remembering the bitter disputes with Paramount and Fox regarding *1900*, preferred to negotiate with the American studios after production was complete.[2] Nevertheless, the American market for *The Last Emperor* was clearly regarded as crucial. The use of Chinese actors speaking American English and the willingness of Hemdale to pay millions of dollars for North American rights are both signs of the continuing influence of the American film industry on world cinema.

Even with these gestures to the American market, *The Last Emperor* must be considered a daring proposition. As a big-budget film without a guaranteed U.S. distributor, it could have been a disaster for its various backers. Further, *The Last Emperor* is a film with few proven commercial assets. Neither Peter O'Toole, its best-known star, nor Bertolucci was a reliable box-office attraction. The film's leading asset turned out to be something intangible: the Western world's fascination with China.

The People's Republic of China had been closed to visitors from the West for decades before a thawing of diplomatic relations in the 1970s. With a renewal of relations between China and the countries of Europe and North America came a tremendous interest in and enthusiasm for all things Chinese. By the mid-1980s, China had become a prestige destination for Western politicians, businessmen, experts, and tourists. The Western visitors were fascinated by China's mixture of an ancient, traditional culture and a new, egalitarian society. *The Last Emperor* cannily encompasses both of these aspects of China. Many early scenes are set in Beijing's Forbidden City, the walled enclave which for hundreds of years housed the emperor and his retainers. Bertolucci was the first Westerner allowed to shoot a fiction film in this legendary place. But *The Last Emperor* also shows a progression from the last days of empire to the Chinese republic, the autocratic rule of Chiang Kai-shek, and eventually to socialism.

The film presents this historical progression via the biography of Aisin-Gioro Pu Yi, who became the last emperor of China in 1908, when he was three. Using a series of flashbacks, Bertolucci shows the adult Pu Yi (played by John Lone) as an inmate in a Chinese Communist prison camp remembering his extraordinary past. Pu Yi abdicated in favor of the Republic in 1912, but lived on in the Forbidden City as an emperor without an empire until 1924. As a teenager, he was greatly influenced by a British tutor, Reginald Johnson (played by Peter O'Toole). In 1924 the ex-emperor and his wives and servants moved to the port city of Tientsin, where he lived under Japanese protection. From 1934 to 1945 he was the Japanese-installed Emperor of Manchukuo (Manchuria), and in that position aided the Japanese in their invasion of China. In 1945 he was captured by the Russians. After five years in a Russian prison camp (not shown in the film), he was transferred to the newly victorious Chinese Communists in 1950. From 1950 to 1959 he was "re-educated" and forced to write a detailed confession of his crimes; this is the frame for the flashbacks. Finally, in the film's last scenes he is shown as a reformed and freed citizen of modern Beijing. Pu Yi died in 1967.

Even more than *Blow-Up*, *The Last Emperor* is a film of multiple meanings which can meet the needs of several audiences. It is, first of all, a spectacle film of a fairly traditional type, a historical epic of China with impressive settings and a huge cast. As a further fillip, many of the settings are authentic: Bertolucci and his cameraman, Vittorio Storaro, give us a marvelous tour of the Forbidden City. The film is also a powerfully sensual experience, with sumptuous colors, sweeping camera movements, and the mysterious ceremonial decors of a highly developed non-Western civilization. There is erotic spectacle as well, although *The Last Emperor* is more restrained than *Last Tango in Paris*. The erotic scenes emphasize diffuse sensuality rather than focusing on a couple. In one scene, for example, a teenaged Pu Yi plays a game of anonymous sexual touching involving a huge sheet of white cloth and a group of eunuchs. Later, this game becomes the model for his first lovemaking with his wife and his secondary consort (all three "hidden" by a sheet).

The Last Emperor is also a film about politics and history. As historical film, it has at least three possible meanings. At a fairly basic level, it is a defense of Chinese Communism. Bertolucci shows the imperial system as exhausted and corrupt, with the eunuchs and other retainers stealing the Forbidden City's treasures for their own benefit. The period between empire and socialism is presented as anarchic and dangerous. This is the era of warlords, of Japanese invasion, of war between the Kuomintang and the Communists. By contrast, the Communist administration is just and serene. The governor of Pu Yi's prison, who is the film's primary authority figure, is shown as thoughtful and compassionate. And the final scenes of Pu Yi working as a gardener in the People's Republic have a calm beauty.

However, *The Last Emperor* can also be seen as presenting an aristocratic point of view. Its most compelling visual images celebrate the imperial court of the Forbidden City. In post–Forbidden City scenes, it sympathizes with Pu Yi's victimization and his problems of identity. One reviewer noted Bertolucci's "Viscontian fascination . . . with the last representatives of a family, of a caste, of a tradition, of a culture."[3] Intellectually, Bertolucci condemns the excesses of empire. Emotionally, his film seems to regret the lost world of palaces, eunuchs, and ladies-in-waiting. Pu Yi is shown as a man who has great difficulty in existing apart from this magical world.

A third historical meaning has to do with the film's insistent metaphor of Pu Yi as an actor, a puppet in a play. Pu Yi is constantly being manipulated—by his retainers, by the Japanese, by the Chinese Communists. As Robert Burgoyne has suggested, history from this point of view is simply a spectacle, a manipulation of the individual to create useful "model images."[4] Pu Yi is important only as a symbol, but his symbolic behavior does have real consequences. For example, his pro-Japanese speeches and gestures in Manchukuo during World War II were filmed by newsreel cameras and used to support the Japanese war effort in China.[5] This third interpretation brings into doubt *The Last*

Emperor's pro-Communist stance, for Pu Yi's last metamorphosis can be seen as one more manipulation that serves the interests of the ruling group.

The Last Emperor is also rich and complex as a psychological parable. Much of the interest of the Forbidden City sequences comes from parallels between the situation of the child emperor and the normal development of a child. A young child raised in a loving family is fed, clothed, and pampered by family members. The child emperor lives in similar conditions, but on a grand scale: he has thousands of retainers catering to his wishes. A maturing child develops new capabilities and new understandings which add to his/her power. Pu Yi, too, develops and explores his powers, for example by running through the compound so that his eunuchs must run behind him. But a maturing child also encounters explicit barriers to his/her autonomy, and realizes his/her powerlessness. This is presented metonymically in *The Last Emperor* by Pu Yi's imprisonment within the Forbidden City's walls. He is the emperor, but he cannot leave.

A psychoanalytical side of Pu Yi's story is that he becomes an emperor at the cost of being separated from his mother and father. He retains his wetnurse as a mother-substitute, then even she is taken from him at age eight. The Forbidden City, with its extravagant riches and its many attendants, is also a kind of mother-substitute. It, too, is lost; Pu Yi is expelled in 1924. Given this series of losses, it is not surprising that Pu Yi tries desperately to regain some vestiges of power. He attempts to become emperor again (in Manchukuo in the 1930s), and to return to the place of his power (in his visit to the Forbidden City in 1967). The loss of his mother explains much about Pu Yi's character. But it is also a universal situation. We all are separated from our mothers and from the magical environments of childhood.

So far *The Last Emperor* has been discussed as a spectacle film, as an historical film, and as a psychological parable. We must add at least one more level: the aesthetic, or (more specifically) the auteurist. Despite its big budget and its emphasis on spectacle, *The Last Emperor* has a number of art-film elements. It is, certainly, a character study, an intimate portrait of a man trapped in a ceremonial role. In observing Pu Yi from age three to age sixty-two, we become aware of his needs, his hopes, and his profound disappointments. The film is also full of ambiguities and enigmas. For example: As emperor of China and/or Manchukuo, did Pu Yi have any freedom of action, real or potential? Did Pu Yi ever love any of those around him (his wife, his secondary consort, his brother, his son, Mr. Johnston)? Did Pu Yi authentically change after nine years of "re-education" in prison? The film's formal and thematic innovations are obvious. Bertolucci and Storaro, masters of the expressive moving camera, enjoy in *The Last Emperor* the pleasures of widescreen photography, a big budget, and a visually splendid subject. Thematically, Bertolucci extends his psycho-socio-sexual outlook to a unique character and a non-Western culture.

The Last Emperor echoes several earlier Bertolucci films. The title evokes two of the director's previous films, *Last Tango in Paris* and *Before the Revolution*. The story of Pu Yi could have been subtitled "Before and After the Revolution." The theme of exploring and giving meaning to the past recalls *The Spider's Strategem*, where a young man seeks out the causes of his father's death in Fascist Italy. The motif of a weak man filmed in a visual context of monumental architecture recalls *The Conformist;* in both films the visual motif represents history's victimization of the individual. But *The Last Emperor* seems most similar to *1900*. Both films are large-scale epics which view major events of the twentieth century through the experiences of their protagonists. Both follow the main characters from extreme youth through old age. Both are structured by flashbacks. The major difference is that *The Last Emperor* is a more organized, more coherent work. *1900* often seems pulled in several directions, and it extends the length and importance of individual scenes at the expense of the whole. Bertolucci describes *1900* as an "infinite" film, a loosely scripted project where production finished without coming to a definitive ending.[6] *The Last Emperor*, on the other hand, was a tightly scripted film where the production schedule was limited by the cost and complexity of filming in China, and by Jeremy Thomas's desire for a two-and-a-half-hour film (American release prints run two hours, forty-six minutes). The flashbacks are under control, and the entire film is focused on the contrast between the Forbidden City and modern Beijing, or in individual terms on Pu Yi, emperor, and Pu Yi, citizen.

Another factor separating *The Last Emperor* from *1900* is that Pu Yi seems to be a composite of that film's two protagonists. In *1900*, Bertolucci's political sympathies lie with the peasants, but he is also fascinated, even obsessed, by the decadence of the landowners. Thus, he is pulled between his main characters, Olmo the peasant and Alfredo the landowner. So much screen time is spent on Alfredo's emotional and erotic adventures that scenes from Olmo's moralistic perspective sometimes seem tacked on. In *The Last Emperor*, Pu Yi begins life as an aristocrat, indeed as a god on earth, but after re-education becomes a worker among workers. He therefore embodies the two poles of *1900* within a single life. This representation of political opposites within biography makes *The Last Emperor* a simpler and easier-to-follow film than *1900*.

The encounter between China and the West is an important dimension of *The Last Emperor.* In Tientsin, Western culture is equated with decadence. Pu Yi, expelled from the Forbidden City, becomes a Westernized playboy under the name Henry Pu Yi. The Tientsin flashback begins with a closeup of Pu Yi in Western dress (tuxedo, slicked-back hair) singing the American song "Am I Blue?" The camera then pulls back to show Pu Yi leaning on a piano, with the piano player accompanying him and a soiree of Europeans listening. The song in this context is an artificial and bizarre lament for a lost "gal" (China?), which shows that Pu Yi the playboy is a superficial construct. Also, the staging of the song suggests the scenes in *To Have and Have Not* and *The Big Sleep* where Lauren Bacall sings at a piano. Even Pu Yi's tenor voice is quite similar to Bacall's. The parallelism of Pu Yi with an apparently tough but actually vulnerable female character suggests a good deal about the ex-emperor's situation. He is passive and victimized, superficially westernized but struggling to find an identity. The limits of his independent, playboy pose are shown when a glowering Japanese official requests that the emperor and his two wives return to the Japanese legation for the evening.

The question of identity reappears on the trip home from the party when Pu Yi's secondary consort tells him that there is no place for her in a westernized environment, and that she wants a divorce. Pu Yi ignores this objection, but the secondary consort takes action. She simply walks out of the Japanese legation and disappears from the story. Unlike Pu Yi and his wife, Wan Jung, who dream about going to the West without ever giving up the comforts of their gilded exile, the secondary consort acts decisively by leaving. Perhaps a filmmaker will someday imagine what happens to her after this moment.[7]

If the West equals decadence in the Tientsin scenes, it has a different meaning in the scenes of Pu Yi conversing with his tutor, Mr. Johnston. Johnston's logical perspective is largely responsible for freeing Pu Yi from the domination of the eunuchs and giving him a measure of self-understanding and autonomy. Under Johnston's influence Pu Yi gets married, expels the eunuchs, and takes command of his private domain. A metonym of Johnston's positive influence on Pu Yi is his insistence that the emperor wear spectacles. Pu Yi is examined by a Western eye specialist, who says the emperor's sight may be endangered if he does not wear corrective lenses. The eunuchs and the high consorts (widows of previous emperors) argue that spectacles would be beneath the dignity of the emperor. Johnston understands that the eunuchs prefer a weak emperor, and might actually be pleased if the emperor went blind. He bluffs and threatens the chief eunuch until the objections to spectacles are dropped. Another symbol of Johnston's influence is the bicycle he acquires for Pu Yi. A bicycle gives the Emperor increased mobility, and therefore greater control over the Forbidden City. It does not, however, change the Emperor's situation of being confined behind walls and therefore essentially irrelevant to the changes taking place in China.

Bicycles reappear in a different context late in the film. Pu Yi, having been freed from prison, pedals to work with thousands of other Chinese. Here the Western invention of the bicycle is not a curiosity given to the Emperor, but rather a labor-saving tool used by the new socialist society. Western technology gains a powerful social utility only with the triumph of Communism.

The scene of Pu Yi bicycling to work is also an interesting representation of freedom. The Emperor of China has been confined and constrained all his life: in the Forbidden City, in Tientsin, in Manchukuo, in Russian and Chinese prisons. Here, as a worker among workers, he is free. There are no walls confining him, no constraints except the rules of social order (e.g., obeying traffic lights) and the requirements of productive work. The same theme is underlined by brief shots of Pu Yi looking with delight at vegetables in a market. This is exactly the kind of experience he could not have as emperor, where every meal was an elaborate ceremonial occasion. Shorn of his power and uniqueness, Pu Yi is, paradoxically, free.

Despite the beauty and originality of these images of freedom, the film maintains some doubt as to whether Pu Yi ever authentically changed, gave up his self-identity as Emperor to become an anonymous citizen. What did Pu Yi actually think about his past during his eight years as a worker in Beijing, 1959–1967? The film does not present Pu Yi's reflections in dialogue at this time, and the few scenes of these years are ambiguous. On the one hand, Pu Yi defends the governor of the prison who is paraded, with other officials, through the streets as a victim of the "Cultural Revolution." He describes his former interrogator as "a teacher." On the other hand, in one of the film's last scenes Pu Yi visits the Forbidden City and sits on the throne. He tells a young boy (the caretaker's son) that he used to live in the Forbidden City, proving this by pulling out from behind the throne the cricket box that he had been given at age three. And in the box, magically, there is a cricket which the little boy allows to escape. Is Pu Yi still, in his own mind, the emperor, returning to his seat of power in the year of his death? Or is the release of the cricket a final symbol of the triumph of the mundane over the ceremonial? *The Last Emperor* ends without resolving the enigma.

This point is important, because *The Last Emperor* as a pro-

Chinese epic centers on a positive image of Pu Yi's reformation. Berto-lucci has declared in interviews that he believes in the usefulness and effectiveness of the Chinese technique of re-educating criminals. He has compared this approach to a "forced psychoanalysis," and has noted his own debt to a psychoanalysis of fifteen years' duration.[8] He has also underscored the specifically Chinese character of this technique, re-lating it to the Confucian belief in the perfectability of man.[9] But Bertolucci's film includes at least a margin of doubt as to whether Pu Yi has changed. And this margin of doubt brings into question the moral superiority of Chinese Communism which the film at one level argues.

For Richard Bernstein, writing in the *New York Times, The Last Emperor*'s ambiguity does not provide an adequate critical analysis of recent Chinese history. Bernstein suggests that the film presents the more or less official position of Chinese Communism. He argues that *The Last Emperor* excuses and whitewashes the imprisonment of mil-lions in Manchurian prison camps, "one of the horrific episodes of re-cent history." According to Bernstein, the Manchurian prisons were grim camps marked by extreme cruelty and deprivation. The physical hardships were made even more terrible by the practice of "absolute" and "ideologically zealous" thought control: "Prisoners were called on to make constant confessions of everyday behavior, a non-stop ritual of submission to authority. They learned that for a prisoner to appeal a sentence meant that he had failed to accept his own guilt."[10] Regarding Pu Yi, Bernstein quotes Lucien Bodard, a journalist who interviewed the ex-emperor in 1956. Bodard found Pu Yi to be a brainwashed and hu-miliated man, "quaking with fear" of his guards.[11] This image of totali-tarian control is a far cry from the gentle re-education presented by *The Last Emperor*.

Bernstein's argument is overstated, but he does bring up some key points. By reasoning from the general status of prisoners in Manchuria, Bernstein has exaggerated the harshness of Pu Yi's imprisonment. Pu Yi was a special prisoner to the communists, who immediately recognized his propaganda value. He received preferential treatment.[12] The contra-dictory views of Pu Yi's re-molding in prison are more problematic. Bodard describes a personality-destroying brainwashing, Bertolucci a calm, slow re-education. The truth is probably somewhere in between. Jean Pasqualini, author of a powerful memoir describing seven years in Chinese prisons, describes many techniques of re-education or brain-washing. They range from learning to parrot the correct ideological phrases to being verbally abused for hours or days by an assembly of one's fellow prisoners.[13]

Bernstein's general point that *The Last Emperor* presents an officially sanctioned view of the People's Republic of China deserves detailed consideration. Bertolucci and Thomas were strikingly dependent on the Chinese in making *The Last Emperor*, and this dependence influenced the film's content. Bertolucci had originally proposed two projects to the Chinese: *Man's Hope*, based on the novel by Malraux, and *From Emperor to Citizen*. He was steered away from *Man's Hope* because of government objections to that novel's interpretation of the Communist Revolution in China. *From Emperor to Citizen*, however, was already a state-endorsed project, since it had been written (by Pu Yi and ghostwriter Li Wenda), published, and translated into many languages with government approval. The film itself absolutely required government cooperation and resources. Bertolucci and Thomas's preliminary research, collaboration with Chinese film companies, choice of locations, and use of extras depended on the goodwill of the Chinese government. The filmmakers' lack of knowledge of Chinese language and culture magnified their reliance on Chinese translators and intermediaries. And, notwithstanding the director's freedom to mold the film's images and to add connotations, the general outline of *The Last Emperor*'s script was approved by the Chinese government. The filmmakers were not speaking for the Chinese, but their work was channeled by dependence on their hosts.

In making *The Last Emperor*, Bertolucci was trying to escape from the commercialism of the West and the constraints of working for American companies. He told John Powers, "I was so depressed by Italy and its consumerism that I could not make another film there."[14] Filming in China seems to have stimulated his imagination; *The Last Emperor* is an emotionally and intellectually powerful film. But filming in China added a new set of constraints to the old set, which did not entirely disappear. On one hand, the American-dominated world film industry still imposed limitations of length, stars, language, and so on. On the other hand, the Chinese government imposed limitations of subject matter and ideology.

By accepting both sets of constraints and cleverly working between them, Bertolucci and his collaborators do gain a measure of freedom. Exploiting the pro-Chinese attitudes of the Western democracies in the mid-1980s, they are able to make a successful film about the decadence of the wealthy and the virtues of communism. Using the Chinese desires for hard currency and international visibility, they become the first Western feature filmmakers to shoot in the Forbidden City. But dependence on the Chinese puts Bertolucci, Thomas et al., in the situation of losing some control of the social and political import of their work.

The production history of *The Last Emperor* suggests at least two general points about the Euro-American art films of the last few years. First, in an era of "globalization," international film productions now involve a broad range of collaborators. For *The Last Emperor*, production partners included Chinese, Japanese, Italian, and British companies. The Asian dimension of international co-production will probably accelerate in the 1990s because of the economic power of Japan and other East Asian nations, and because of the ongoing cultural mix which has made futons and sushi popular in the United States, and baseball a leading sport in Japan. A second point to be stressed is that working with new production partners does not provide a utopian creative freedom. The exotic images, sounds, and stories of China in *The Last Emperor* come with a price—the channeling of the film's ideas by the Chinese government.

11. Final Comments

For each of the five sample films, the synthesis of Europe and America, art and entertainment is in some way difficult, contested, problematic. In making *Contempt*, Godard crafted a meditative art film by working *against* the needs and expectations of his producers, Carlo Ponti and Joe Levine. The entire film is based on a misunderstanding. *Blow-Up* enjoyed a greater harmony between director (Antonioni) and producer (Ponti again, in collaboration with MGM). However, the film can be perceived, or received, as all surface—fashionable mod London, cool sex, cool jazz—neglecting the critical attitude Antonioni brings to this surface material. Pasolini's *The Canterbury Tales* is marked by an even more serious split between directorial "writing" and audience "reading." The open and diverse sexuality in Pasolini's film has a socially critical and contestatory dimension which some audiences have ignored, thus making the film into a more or less pornographic work. However, this same film has won a prestigious award (Golden Bear at the Berlin Film Festival, 1972) and has elicited thoughtful, positive critiques, so the film's originality and its challenging elements are evidently accessible to some viewers. For *Paris, Texas*, the conflict lies between making a hyper-American film and maintaining links to Europe, the art film, and director Wim Wenders' previous films. The title *Paris, Texas* embodies the tension between these two objectives. Of the five films analyzed in the case study chapters, *The Last Emperor* is probably the most successful at integrating the art film with commercial values (*Blow-Up* would be second). However, *The Last Emperor's* balancing act—between Hollywood, Chinese Communism, and the individualist aesthetic of the art film—did lead to compromises in the film.

The double nature of the five films, their working between art and entertainment, can also be seen as an achievement. All five of the films attempt to carve out an independent space within the structure of international film production. Though this space is provisional and contested, it does provide opportunities to make films outside the norms of the art film and the Hollywood entertainment film. The success of the art film gives its leading directors some leverage in working for, or with, the American-dominated international film industry. In Gramscian terms, the interaction between two overlapping hegemonies—the powerful American motion picture industry and the less powerful European industry—leads to a certain number of contradictions and ambiguities, and thus to creative opportunities. Is film an art, or is it strictly an entertainment industry? Should films be subsidized, or left to the market economy? Should films be cross-cultural in content, or only in distribution? Should cultural hegemony be a hidden issue, or a subject explicitly addressed by internationally produced and financed films? Such ambiguities provide a starting point for original and creative work.

The "independence" which Euro-American art films strive for is clearly period-specific. In the first important period of Euro-American art films, approximately 1960–1973, there was some opportunity to make films distinct from Hollywood models because of the art film's expanding popularity and the importance of European markets to American film companies. In social-political terms, critical and alternative filmmaking was possible and in some cases even profitable in the United States and Western Europe because of the rapid social changes and the polarization (Vietnam War, race relations, feminism, sexual "revolution," generation gap) of the period. *Contempt* was made near the beginning of this era. It criticizes the American capitalist power represented by the Jack Palance character in an isolated, existentialist way. Also, the Brigitte Bardot character cannot articulate her disgust with her husband's entry into the Hollywood producer's world. The film is proto-Marxist and proto-feminist, but it is also marked by a nostalgia for Hollywood cinema (appearance of Fritz Lang as a figure of tradition, use of the melodrama structure, references to Howard Hawks and Vincente Minnelli). In *Blow-Up*, we enter the very different world of a counterculture where London's young and unconventional artistic set has achieved both freedom and success.[1] The isolated critique of dominant capitalism has become an alternative lifestyle, in only a few years. But Antonioni shows that the apparent freedom of his central character is limited by the norms and horizons of his social group; the unconventional becomes a new orthodoxy.[2]

In *The Canterbury Tales*, the counterculture of the 1960s is represented obliquely, in the peasant culture of medieval England. Pasolini presents sexuality in *The Canterbury Tales* as personally liberating, but he rejects the linkage made by 1960s popular culture between sexuality and political liberation. Instead, Pasolini's picture of medieval England shows a complex interweaving of sexuality and repression, eros and thanatos. There is a desperation in the erotic encounters of *The Canter-*

bury Tales which suggests Pasolini's distance from the naive hopes of the 1960s: characters couple to momentarily hold off death.

With *Paris, Texas* (1984) and *The Last Emperor* (1987), we have entered another era, a period of motion picture history thoroughly dominated by high-budget Hollywood entertainment machines. Wenders responds to this era by ignoring it, making a small-scale film about individual and family conflicts. For the dreams of the sixties, he substitutes the basic problem of sustaining relationships with those you love. Bertolucci, more ambitious, films an exotic spectacle of incredible proportions while maintaining interests in character and theme, in psychoanalysis and history. Although Bertolucci himself is a child of the sixties, in this film the themes of counterculture and resistance are muted. Pu Yi's ineffectual efforts to assert himself as an individual, a controlling subject, are swept away by the tides of history. But perhaps even the attempt to stand against one's socially given role is a positive stance in the conservative 1980s.

There is no sure recipe for making a successful Euro-American art film, and even those recipes that do exist are period-bound. In the 1960s and 1970s, a combination of sexual explicitness, social insight, and artistic prestige brought critical and box-office success to *Never on Sunday, La dolce vita, Blow-Up, The Damned,* and *Last Tango in Paris. The Canterbury Tales* and *1900* were released near the end of the cycle, and did not achieve the same success. More recently, *The Last Emperor*'s originality of subject matter and style swept the Academy Awards of 1987, and several European-financed English-language films have been very successful with European audiences (*Paris, Texas, The Big Blue, The Last Emperor, Bagdad Cafe, The Name of the Rose*). But even Bernardo Bertolucci and Jeremy Thomas, director and producer of *The Last Emperor,* have not found a sure-fire formula for success. Their latest film, *The Sheltering Sky,* a big-budget exotic spectacle, was a huge commercial failure in the United States.

European-financed, English-language films seem to be an established part of world cinema. They may create some sort of Euro-sector, a substantial body of English-language films appealing especially to European audiences. It is more likely, given European and Asian investments in Hollywood companies, that the Hollywood film industry will gradually grow more cosmopolitan. The American, European, and Japanese film industries will develop ever-closer ties, and American-made films will become at least slightly more sensitive to foreign audiences. The ongoing economic integration of the EEC will add to the potential for European-financed movies, but will probably not lead to high-budget films in French, German, or Italian. Instead, English will be confirmed as the language of international film production. Eastern Europe will provide new opportunities for co-productions and film marketing. Indeed, some co-productions involving Eastern Europe, Western Europe, and the United States are already underway, with the Americans and West Europeans providing capital, the East Europeans facilities and crews. With all the changes, Hollywood-style entertainment will maintain its dominance of world markets. The Euro-American art film will continue to exist in the cracks and contradictions of this "new" Hollywood.

The films which have been studied in this book can be seen as a special case of the burgeoning "international cinema." By "international cinema" I do not mean the compendium of discrete national cinemas that is the subject of film-history textbooks, but rather the blends, overlaps, and hegemonies of national cinemas that are so typical of the world film industry of the last forty years. The Euro-American art film is only one manifestation of the blurring of the lines of national cinemas. It is, however, a particularly exciting example of this blurring because of the quality of the films, and because of the cultural conflicts expressed as the art film meets Hollywood.

A broader history of the internationalization of cinema would have to consider such phenomena as the privileged relationship between British and Hollywood cinemas, the virtues and dangers of European co-productions, the impact of a rapidly changing television industry on world film production, the cross-cultural import of the Italian Western and of other commercial genres (including pornography), the sponsorship of Third World filmmakers by France and other European countries, and the increasing entry of Asian, South American, and East European filmmakers and film industries into the American-dominated world film industry. Both economic and cultural histories of the new internationalism are needed. My book's foray into this uncharted territory will, I hope, inspire others to investigate international aspects of film history and current film practice.

Notes

INTRODUCTION

1. Geoffrey Nowell-Smith, "But Do We Need It?" in Martyn Auty and Nick Roddick, eds., *British Cinema Now*, p. 154.
2. Guglielmo Biraghi, "Diverse Batch of Venice Entries Bound Only by Literary Origins," *Variety*, August 24, 1988.
3. David Bordwell, Janet Staiger, and Kristin Thompson, *The Classical Hollywood Cinema*, p. 10.
4. Both definitions are paraphrased from Raymond Williams, *Keywords*, p. 80.
5. Williams, *Keywords*, p. 80; Williams, *The Sociology of Culture*, p. 13.
6. See especially Thomas Guback, *The International Film Industry*, and Guback, "Film and Cultural Pluralism," *Journal of Aesthetic Education* 5, no. 2 (1971): 35–51.
7. Andrew Sarris uses the metaphor of "forest critics" and "tree critics" in *The American Cinema*, pp. 20–21.

1. THE ART FILM

1. Mike Budd discusses the beginnings of art film exhibition in New York in "The National Board of Review and the Early Art Cinema in New York: *The Cabinet of Dr. Caligari* as Affirmative Culture," *Cinema Journal* 26, no. 1 (1986): 8. Daniel and Michel Serceau describe the first Parisian art film theaters in "Le Mouvement art et essai en France: Quelle signification culturelle et économique?" *Image et Son* 339 (1979): 92.
2. David Bordwell, "The Art Cinema as a Mode of Film Practice," *Film Criticism* 4, no. 1 (1979): 57–60.
3. Ibid., p. 60.
4. Steve Neale, "Art Cinema as Institution," *Screen* 22, no. 1 (1981): 11–39.
5. Ibid., p. 15.
6. Dudley Andrew, *Film in the Aura of Art*, pp. 3–15, 193–201.
7. This chapter does not pretend to such completeness. I will limit myself to describing the art film in relation to the United States and Western Europe.

8. Serceau and Serceau, "Le Mouvement art et essai . . . ," p. 97.
9. Guy Phelps, "Art-House," *Sight and Sound* 53, no. 1 (1983–1984): 12–14.
10. This seems to be changing. See my Chapter 8, "Pasolini's *The Canterbury Tales* . . . "
11. See Arthur Mayer, *Merely Colossal* (New York: Simon and Schuster, 1953), p. 233. Richard Griffith expresses this same idea, then questions it, in "European Films and American Audiences," *Saturday Review* 34, no. 2 (January 13, 1951): 85.
12. Michael F. Mayer, *Foreign Films on American Screens*, pp. 1–3.
13. Ibid., p. 3.
14. Robert B. Ray, *A Certain Tendency in the Hollywood Cinema, 1930–1980*, pp. 138–141.
15. François Truffaut, "Une Certaine Tendance du cinéma français," *Cahiers du Cinéma* 31 (1954): 15–29; Truffaut, "Aimer Fritz Lang," *Cahiers du Cinéma* 31 (1954): 52–53.
16. John E. Twomey, "Some Considerations on the Rise of the Art-Film Theater," *Quarterly of Film, Radio and Television* 10, no. 3 (1956): 240.
17. Tim Pulleine mentions Roger Vadim's admiration for *East of Eden* (starring James Dean). " . . . And Vadim Created Women," *Movies of the Fifties*, edited by Ann Lloyd (London: Orbis, 1982), p. 170.
18. Figures taken from Jean-Claude Batz, *A propos de la crise de l'industrie du cinéma*, pp. 14, 21.
19. Cobbett Steinberg, *Reel Facts*, (New York: Vintage, 1978), p. 371.
20. Fred Hift, "Foreign Films Find U.S. Gold," *Variety*, April 9, 1958; "Foreign Films 'Made It' in America during 1959, Theatre Owners Told," *Variety*, November 11, 1959; Vincent Canby, "Film Imports on a Seesaw," *Variety*, May 8, 1963. The 1957 figures exclude "several important American productions shot in Britain and technically British." The 1961 figures, on the other hand, include such technically British (qualifying for Eady fund subsidy) films as *Guns of Navarone*, *Swiss Family Robinson*, and *The World of Suzy Wong*, which together earned nearly $25,000,000 of the $69,000,000 gross for that year.
21. "U.S. Majors Lead N.Y. Arties," *Variety*, September 9, 1964.

2. ECONOMIC LINKS

1. The history of American expansion to a world-dominant position in film exports is presented in detail by Kristin Thompson, *Exporting Entertainment*.
2. "Black Cloud of Television Thickens for Europe's Cinema Operators: Now Have 12,792,805 Video Sets," *Variety*, October 8, 1958.
3. See Kristin Thompson on "Film Europe." Thompson, *Exporting Entertainment*, pp. 112–117.
4. *International Motion Picture Almanac 1989*, p. 25A.
5. Nine hundred and twelve feature films were produced in India in

1985, an astonishing figure. *Unesco Yearbook 1987*, (Paris: UNESCO, 1987), p. 9.4.

6. Peter Besas, *Behind the Spanish Lens*, p. 54.

7. Batz, *A propos de la crise . . .* , p. 58.

8. Vincent Canby, "American Films That Can't Go Home," *Variety*, May 24, 1961.

9. "U.S. Majors Show New Interest in Backing Art Pix," *Variety*, November 28, 1962.

10. Cited by Umberto Rossi, "Italie: Le Règne du dollar," *Ecran* 31 (1974): 5.

11. See Alexander Walker, *Hollywood U.K.*, for an excellent account of Anglo-American film collaborations of the 1960s.

12. Guback, "Cultural Identity and Film in the European Economic Community," *Cinema Journal* 14, no. 1 (1974): 4.

13. Theatrical admissions went up dramatically in Great Britain between 1985 and 1990, thanks in part to the building of American-style multiplex theaters. Total admissions in France and Italy declined during the same period. Combining figures for these three major markets reveals no net gain. *International Motion Picture Almanac* 1987, 1991, 1992.

14. Terry Ilott, "Yank Pix Flex Pecs in New Euro Arena," *Variety*, August 19, 1991.

15. John Marcon, Jr., "Dream Factory to the World," *Forbes*, May 12, 1991.

3. THE EURO-AMERICAN ART FILM: DEFINITION

1. The two key articles which began the critical debate on film noir in the United States were Paul Schrader's, "Notes on Film Noir," *Film Comment* 8, no. 1 (1972): 8–13; and Raymond Durgnat's, "Paint It Black: The Family Tree of Film Noir," *Film Comment* 10, no. 6 (1974): 6–7. An earlier version of Durgnat's article had appeared in the British journal *Cinema* in 1970.

2. Dubbing normally uses a standardized spoken Italian which is only now beginning to correspond to the way Italians actually speak. Dubbing can also be used to give characters the accent of a particular region and social class.

3. Geoffrey Nowell-Smith, "Italy *sotto voce*," *Sight and Sound* 37, no. 3 (1968): 147.

4. Nick Roddick, "If the United States Spoke Spanish, Then We Would Have a Film Industry," in Auty and Roddick, eds., *British Cinema Now*, p. 5.

5. In 1977, Polanski left the United States for France in order to avoid serving a prison sentence (he was convicted of having sexual relations with a minor). However, many of his English-language European films were made *before* 1977.

6. Thomas Schatz, *Hollywood Genres*, p. 14.

7. William C. Siska, "The Art Film," in Wes Gehring, ed., *Handbook of American Film Genres*, pp. 353–368; Dudley Andrew, *Concepts in Film Theory*, p. 121.
8. Bordwell, "The Art Cinema as a Mode of Film Practice," pp. 56–64.
9. Andrew, *Concepts in Film Theory*, p. 110.

4. THE EURO-AMERICAN ART FILM: HISTORY

1. Douglas Gomery, "Economic Struggle and Hollywood Imperialism: Europe Converts to Sound," *Yale French Studies* 60 (1980): 83–84.
2. Peter Bondanella, "America and the Postwar Italian Cinema," *Rivisti di studi italiani* 2 (1984): 108.
3. Peter Brunette, *Roberto Rossellini*, pp. 363–364, n. 4.
4. Two additional Rossellini-Bergman features, *Joan of Arc at the Stake* (1954) and *Fear* (1954), are not discussed because I have been unable to view them.
5. Brunette, *Roberto Rossellini*, p. 117.
6. Raymond Durgnat, *Jean Renoir*, pp. 274, 285–286.
7. A United Artists' internal memo from Charles Smadja to Arthur Krim, dated July 29, 1959, lays out the financial terms for production of the film. UA was to put up $125,000, the Greek co-producer $50,000. Dassin and Mercouri deferred their salaries until the film had recouped its expenses. United Artists Collection, Wisconsin Center for Film and Theater Research.
8. Production details on *The Leopard* come primarily from Gaia Servadio, *Luchino Visconti: A Biography*, p. 178.
9. Kenneth Turan and Stephen Zito, *Sinema*, pp. 52, 57.
10. Hank Werba, "Italo-U.S. Co-prod Trend Continues," *Variety*, January 10, 1968.
11. Aldo Tassone, *Le Cinéma italien parle* (Paris: Edilig, 1982), p. 115.
12. T. Jefferson Kline finds the dominant pattern of *1900* to be repetition, not revolution. *Bertolucci's Dream Loom*, pp. 140–143.
13. "PEA," *Variety*, May 7, 1980.
14. Diane Jacobs, *Hollywood Renaissance*.
15. Ingmar Bergman, *The Magic Lantern*, p. 131.
16. Steve Chagollan, "Filmmakers in Focus: Wim Wenders," *Hollywood Reporter*, June 12, 1988.
17. Peter Biskind, "Blockbusters," in Mark Crispin Miller, ed., *Seeing through Movies* (New York: Pantheon, 1990), pp. 124–125. Spielberg's choice of a lavish adaptation of *Peter Pan* as his latest project confirms the acuity of Biskind's argument.

5. CULTURAL DOMINANCE OR CULTURAL MIX

1. Jeremy Tunstall, *The Media Are American*, pp. 63, 137–143; Stewart Brand, *The Media Lab* (New York: Penguin, 1988), p. 236.
2. Antonio Gramsci, *Selections from the Prison Notebooks of Antonio Gramsci*, pp. 57–59. See also 55n.
3. Ibid., pp. 12, 160–161, 210, 238–239; Walter Adamson, *Hegemony*

and Revolution, pp. 170–179; Raymond Williams, *Marxism and Literature*, pp. 108–114. Williams uses the term "counter-hegemony," pp. 113–114.

4. Antonio Gramsci, *Selections from Cultural Writings*, p. 209.

5. Ibid., p. 211.

6. Ibid., p. 209.

7. Geoffrey Nowell-Smith uses this same passage of Gramsci to comment on the role of American film in Great Britain. Nowell-Smith, "But Do We Need It?" in *British Cinema Now*, p. 151.

8. James Monaco, "Images and Sounds as Cultural Commodities," *Sight and Sound* 49, no. 4 (1980): 211. Herbert Gans, "Hollywood Films on British Screens," *Social Problems* 9 (1962). Reprinted in Peter Davison et al., eds., *Literary Taste, Culture and Mass Communication, vol. 5: Literature and Society*, pp. 278–281.

9. Francesco Rosi, Statement in *La Biennale: The Cinema in the Eighties* (Venice: Editions La Biennale di Venezia, 1980), p. 45.

10. All the foreign films discussed are European. "Are Foreign Films Better?" (Symposium), *Saturday Review*, December 24, 1960, pp. 43–53.

11. Peter Bart, "Europe's Successes Worry Hollywood," *New York Times*, September 20, 1965; Bart, "The Excitement Is All from Europe," *New York Times*, April 13, 1966; Bart, "Where the Action Isn't," *New York Times*, July 31, 1966.

12. Quoted by Diane Jacobs, *Hollywood Renaissance*, p. 99.

13. Todd McCarthy, "Speed of Light," *Film Comment* 25, no. 5 (1989): 32–45. McCarthy lists Storaro, Almendros, Nykvist, and Muller in the top rank of cinematographers currently working in American (or English-language) cinema, along with Haskell Wexler (USA), Chris Menges (UK), John Seale (Australia), and David Watkin (UK).

14. Stanley Kauffmann, "The Film Generation: Celebration and Concern," in *A World on Film*, pp. 415–419.

15. Williams, *Marxism and Literature*, p. 114.

16. Colin MacCabe, "English Literature in a Global Context," in *English in the World*, pp. 44–45.

17. Philippe Carcassone and Jacques Fieschi, "Jean-Luc Godard" (interview), *Cinématographe* 61 (1981): 8.

18. Bertolucci considered himself "French" because of an affinity to French cinema. Franca Faldini and Goffredo Fofi, eds., *Il cinema italiano d'oggi* (Milano: Arnoldo Mondadori, 1984), p. 655.

19. See, for example, Michelangelo Antonioni, *Techniquement douce*, trans. Anna Buresi (Paris: Albatros, 1977).

6. ART AND COMMERCE IN *CONTEMPT*

1. Jean-Luc Godard, *Introduction à une véritable histoire du cinéma*, p. 85; Herbert Feinstein, "An Interview with Jean-Luc Godard," *Film Quarterly* 17, no. 3 (1964): 9.

2. This was a large budget for a French film in 1963. Most of the early New Wave films were made for $100,000 or less.

3. Glenys Roberts, *Bardot* (New York: St. Martin's, 1984), pp. 189–190.

4. "Early 'New Wave' Producer Airs Ideas," *Variety*, April 3, 1963.

5. A copy of this unpublished script is in the Fritz Lang Collection, Department of Special Collections, Doheny Library, University of Southern California.

6. Godard, *Contempt* script (104 pages), University of Southern California, pp. 54–56. Another script draft for *Contempt*—69 pages, also at University of Southern California—does provide some dialogue for the apartment scene between Bardot and Piccoli.

7. One of the ambiguities of *Contempt* is whether *The Odyssey* should be considered Prokosch's film or Lang's film. This suggests the additional question of whether *Contempt* itself is a Godard film or a Ponti-Levine-De Beauregard film.

8. Gene Moskowitz, "*Le Mépris*" (review), *Variety*, January 1, 1964.

9. Godard, *Introduction à une véritable histoire*, pp. 85–86.

10. Feinstein, "Interview with Jean-Luc Godard," p. 9. This interview was conducted in October, 1963.

11. Martin Walsh, "Godard and Me: Jean-Pierre Gorin Talks," in *The Brechtian Aspect of Radical Cinema*, edited by Keith M. Griffiths (London: British Film Institute, 1981), p. 122. Gorin was not a collaborator of Godard until 1968, so his anecdote about *Contempt* would be hearsay.

12. On the alterations supervised by Ponti, see Adriano Aprà, "*Le Mépris* e *Il disprezzo*," *Filmcritica* 151–152 (1964): 611–613; Michele Mancini, *Godard*, pp. 75–79; Julia Lesage, *Jean-Luc Godard: A Guide to References and Resources*, p. 55.

13. Aprà, "*Le Mépris* e *Il disprezzo*," p. 611.

14. Godard, *Introduction à une véritable histoire*, p. 86.

15. Vincent Canby, "Hollywood Woos Foreign Talent," *New York Times*, November 26, 1966.

7. *BLOW-UP,* SWINGING LONDON, AND THE FILM GENERATION

1. Francis Wyndham, "The Modelmakers," *London Sunday Times Magazine*, May 10, 1964.

2. Alexander Walker, *Hollywood U.K.: The British Film Industry in the Sixties*, pp. 316–317, 320–322.

3. British playwright Edward Bond was added to the scriptwriting team to help with English-language dialogue.

4. Antonioni specifically refers to Elizabeth Taylor and Franco Zeffirelli. Rex Reed, "After the 'Blow-Up,' a Close-Up," *New York Times*, January 1, 1967.

5. Publicity release, *Blow-Up*, prepared for Director's Guild of America screening, Los Angeles, December 14, 1966.

6. See, for example, Joseph Morgenstern, "How De-Dramatizer Works," *New York Herald Tribune*, April 2, 1961; Ian Dallas, "Antonioni on Seeking Love," *Observer* (London), February 4, 1962.

7. Andrew Tudor, "Death Valley," *Cinema* (London) 6–7 (1970): 27–28.

8. "Approval Denied to Antonioni Film," *New York Times*, December 17, 1966.
9. "MGM Prunes Print on QT," *Variety*, January 26, 1967.
10. Memo, Geoffrey Shurlock to Michael Linden, November 23, 1966; Letter, Michael Linden to Dan Terrell, November 25, 1966; Letter, Terrell to Linden, November 28, 1966; Letter, Robert Vogel to Shurlock, January 27, 1967; File Memo, Ralph Hetzel, January 31, 1967. G. Shurlock was head of the Production Code Administration. M. Linden was head of the Code for Advertising. D. Terrell and R. Vogel were MGM executives. R. Hetzel was a PCA employee.

All letters and memos listed in this note are from the MPAA Collection, Margaret Herrick Library, Academy of Motion Picture Arts and Sciences.
11. "Gross of $7 Million," *Hollywood Reporter*, May 23, 1967.
12. "'Blow-Up' Calms Down; No 'Criminal Angle,'" *Variety*, November 11, 1967; Andrew Rhodes, "Censorship Blowup over 'Blow-Up,'" *Los Angeles Times*, November 5, 1967.
13. Kauffmann, "The Film Generation," pp. 415–417.
14. "'Blow-Up' Able to Rile Baltimore," *Variety*, March 8, 1967.
15. Pauline Kael, "Tourist in the City of Love," *New Republic*, February 11, 1967, pp. 30, 32–35; "Correspondence," *New Republic*, February 25, 1967, pp. 39–41.
16. "Playboy Interview: Michelangelo Antonioni," *Playboy*, November 1967, pp. 77–88.
17. Charles Eidsvik, *Cineliteracy*, pp. 229–230.
18. Kauffmann, "The Film Generation," pp. 426–427.

8. PASOLINI'S *THE CANTERBURY TALES:*
THE ESTRANGEMENT OF AN ENGLISH CLASSIC

1. Quoted by Giacomo Gambetti, "Per una 'Trilogia popolare, libera, erotica,'" *Cineforum* 13.121 (1973): 221.
2. Hank Werba, "Alberto Grimaldi Emerges as Italo Strong Man in Field of Quality Films," *Variety*, March 21, 1973.
3. Pier Paolo Pasolini, Press Conference at the Berlin Film Festival, 1972. Transcribed in Paul Willemin, ed., *Pier Paolo Pasolini*, pp. 72–73.
4. Pier Paolo Pasolini, *Pasolini on Pasolini: Interviews with Oswald Stack*, p. 39.
5. The tales of erotic exchange are the Merchant's Tale, the Cook's Tale, the Miller's Tale, the Wife of Bath's Prologue, and the Reeve's Tale. The tales of death and damnation are the Friar's Tale, the Pardoner's Tale, the Summoner's Tale, and the Summoner's Prologue.
6. The friar's dream of hell (the Summoner's Prologue) was shot on the slopes of Mount Aetna. Pasolini, Berlin Press Conference, in Willemin, *Pasolini*, p. 73.
7. Claude Beylie, "Pasolini l'exorciseur," in *Pier Paolo Pasolini* (Paris: Seghers, 1973), p. 127.

8. The term "Italianized" is borrowed from Giacomo Gambetti, who discusses Pasolini's "Italianization" of Chaucer, with the mix of dialects as his primary example. Gambetti, "Per una 'Trilogia,'" p. 226.

9. André Cornand and Dominique Maillet, "Entretien avec Pier Paolo Pasolini," *Image et Son* 267 (1973): 84.

10. Ibid., p. 85; Alessandri Gennari, "Conversazione con Pier Paolo Pasolini," *Filmcritica* 247 (1974): 281; Claude-Michel Cluny, "Rencontre avec Pasolini," *Cinéma* (Paris) 164 (1972): 57.

11. Gambetti, "Per una 'Trilogia,'" pp. 224, 227.

12. Robert Kolker, *The Altering Eye*, p. 225.

13. Mira Liehm, *Passion and Defiance: Film in Italy from 1942 to the Present*, p. 260.

14. Pier Paolo Pasolini, "Trilogy of Life Rejected," in *Lutheran Letters*, pp. 49–52. This essay originally appeared in *Corriere della Sera*, November 9, 1975.

9. *PARIS, TEXAS,* AN AMERICAN DREAM

1. Kathe Geist, *The Cinema of Wim Wenders*, p. 82.

2. Herbert Achternbusch, "Amerika: Report to the Goethe Institute," in Eric Rentschler, ed., *West German Filmmakers on Film: Visions and Voices* (New York: Holmes and Meier, 1988), p. 209.

3. Don Ranvaud, "Paris, Texas to Sydney, Australia," *Sight and Sound* 53, no. 4 (1984): 247.

4. Sam Shepard, *Motel Chronicles and Hawk Moon*, p. 85.

5. Gaylyn Studlar, "*Paris, Texas*" (review), in Frank Magill, ed., *Magill's Film Annual 1985*, (New Jersey: Salem Press, 1985), p. 360.

6. Wim Wenders, *Emotion Pictures: Reflections on the Cinema*, pp. 116–117.

7. Kathe Geist says "the portrayal of sustained emotion between a man and a woman is a breakthrough for Wenders." She then criticizes the director for not including the woman's point of view (Jane's point of view) in *Paris, Texas*. Geist, *Cinema of Wim Wenders*, p. 118.

8. Ibid., p. 118.

9. Ibid., p. 118.

10. Ranvaud, "Paris, Texas to Sydney, Australia," p. 249.

11. Michel Ciment, *Passeport pour Hollywood*, p. 367.

10. *THE LAST EMPEROR:* PLEASURES AND DANGERS OF THE EXOTIC

1. William K. Knoedelseder Jr., "Making 'Emperor' in China an Epic Job of Financing," *Los Angeles Times*, February 1, 1988.

2. Jean-Claude Carrière, "Bertolucci à Pékin," *Cahiers du Cinéma* 392 (1987): 64.

3. Alain Philippon, "Le Vaste Pays de l'âme," *Cahiers du Cinéma* 401 (1987): 6.

4. Robert Burgoyne, "*The Last Emperor*: The Stages of History," *SubStance* 59 (1989): 93.

5. Ibid., pp. 97–99.

6. Carrière, "Bertolucci à Pékin," p. 61.

7. The story of Wen Hsiu, the secondary consort, is less romantic in Pu Yi's autobiography than in Bertolucci's film. According to Paul Kramer's edited version of the autobiography, Wen Hsiu divorced the ex-emperor, obtaining an alimony of fifty thousand dollars. She eventually became a schoolteacher and never remarried. Henry Pu Yi, *The Last Manchu*, pp. 156–157.

8. Alain Philippon and Serge Toubiana, "Sur les traces de Pu Yi" (interview with Bertolucci), *Cahiers du Cinéma* 401 (1987): 10.

9. Carrière, "Bertolucci à Pékin," p. 60.

10. Richard Bernstein, "'The Last Emperor' Truth or Propaganda," *New York Times*, May 8, 1988.

11. Lucien Bodard, "The Survivor of the Forbidden City," *Encounter* 80, no. 3 (1988): 42–43.

12. Edward Behr, *The Last Emperor*, pp. 293–294; Philippon and Toubiana, "Sur les traces de Pu Yi," p. 9.

13. Bao Ruo-Wang (Jean Pasqualini) and Rudolph Chelminski, *Prisoner of Mao*, pp. 51–53, 58–62.

14. John Powers, "Bernardo Needs a Hit," *L. A. Weekly*, November 20, 1987.

11. FINAL COMMENTS

1. Andrew Tudor has astutely applied the concept of "countercultures" to *Blow-Up*. Tudor, "Death Valley," *Cinema* (London) 6–7 (1970): 28.

2. "Thomas (the photographer) leads an existence that is regulated like a ceremonial." Michelangelo Antonioni, "Una intensa emozione che la troupe interrompe," *Cinema Nuovo* 277 (1982): 7.

Filmography: Euro-American Art Films

This filmography is lengthy but by no means exhaustive. It includes the films discussed in Chapter 4 plus a few additional titles. Some wonderfully talented filmmakers—e.g., Milos Forman, Jerzy Skolimowsky, Sergio Leone—have been left out because they do not fit the parameters outlined in Chapter 3.

Adventures of Robinson Crusoe (1954). Production company: Ultramar. Director: Luis Buñuel. Screenplay: Phillip Roll and Luis Buñuel, based on the novel by Daniel Defoe. Cinematography: Alex Phillips. Editors: Carlos Savage, Alberto Valenzuela. Cast: Dan O'Herlihy, James Fernandez, Felipe De Alba, Chel Lopez.

Alamo Bay (1985). Production company: Tri-Star. Director: Louis Malle. Screenplay: Alice Arlen. Producers: Louis Malle, Vincent Malle. Cinematography: Curtis Clark. Editor: James Bruce. Music: Ry Cooder. Cast: Ed Harris, Amy Madigan, Ho Nguyen.

Alice in the Cities (1973). Production companies: Filmverlag der Autoren, Westdeutscher Rundfunk. Director: Wim Wenders. Screenplay: Wim Wenders, Veith von Furstenburg. Producer: Peter Gende. Cinematography: Robbie Muller. Editor: Peter Przygodda. Music: Chuck Berry, Canned Heat, Deep Purple, Count Five, Stories, Gustav Mahler. Cast: Rudiger Vogler, Yella Rottlander, Lisa Kreuzer.

The American Friend (1977). Production companies: Road Movies Filmproduktion, Films du Losange, Wim Wenders Produktion, Westdeutscher Rundfunk. Director: Wim Wenders. Screenplay: Wim Wenders, based on the novel *Ripley's Game* by Patricia Highsmith. Producer: Michael Wiedemann, Pierre Cottrell. Cinematography: Robbie Muller. Editor: Peter Przygodda. Music: Jurgen Knieper, the Kinks. Cast: Bruno Ganz, Dennis Hopper, Lisa Kreuzer, Gérard Blain, Nicholas Ray, Samuel Fuller.

Another Man, Another Chance (1977). Production companies: Films 13, Films Ariane, United Artists. Director: Claude Lelouch. Screenplay: Claude Lelouch. Producer: Alexandre Mnouchkine, Georges Dancigers.

Cinematography: Jacques Lefrançois, Stanley Cortez, Claude Lelouch. Editors: Georges Klotz, Fabien Tordjmann. Music: Francis Lai. Cast: James Caan, Genevieve Bujold, Francis Huster, Jennifer Warren, Susan Tyrrell, Jacques Villeret.

Atlantic City (1981). Production company: Paramount. Director: Louis Malle. Screenplay: John Guare. Producer: Denis Heroux. Cinematography: Richard Ciupka. Music: Michel Legrand. Cast: Burt Lancaster, Susan Sarandon, Kate Reid, Michel Piccoli.

Bagdad Cafe (1988). Production company: Pelemele Film. Director: Percy Adlon. Screenplay: Percy Adlon, Eleonore Adlon, Christopher Doherty. Producers: Percy Adlon, Eleonore Adlon. Cinematography: Bernd Heinl. Editor: Norbert Herzner. Music: Bob Telson. Cast: Marianne Sagebrecht, C. C. H. Pounder, Jack Palance, Christine Kaufmann.

Barfly (1987). Production company: Cannon. Director: Barbet Schroeder. Screenplay: Charles Bukowski. Producers: Barbet Schroeder, Fred Roos, Tom Luddy. Cinematography: Robby Muller. Editor: Eva Gardos. Cast: Mickey Rourke, Faye Dunaway, Alice Krige, Jack Nance.

The Big Blue (1987). Production companies: Films du Loup, Gaumont, Columbia. Director: Luc Besson. Screenplay: Luc Besson, Robert Garland, Marilyn Goldin, Jacques Mayol, Marc Perrier. Producer: Patrice Ledoux. Cinematography: Carlo Vareni. Editor: Olivier Mauffroy. Music: Bill Conti. Cast: Jean-Marc Barr, Rosanna Arquette, Jean Reno, Paul Shenar.

Blow-Up (1966). Production company: MGM. Director: Michelangelo Antonioni. Screenplay: Michelangelo Antonioni, Tonino Guerra from a short story by Julio Cortázar. Producer: Carlo Ponti. Cinematography: Carlo di Palma. Editor: Frank Clarke. Music: Herbie Hancock. Cast: David Hemmings, Vanessa Redgrave, Sarah Miles, John Castle.

Breathless (alternate title *A bout de souffle*) (1959). Production companies: Imevia Films, Société Nouvelle de Cinéma. Director: Jean-Luc Godard. Screenplay: Jean-Luc Godard, from an original treatment by François Truffaut. Producer: Georges de Beauregard. Cinematography: Raoul Coutard. Editor: Cecile Decugis. Music: Martial Solal, Mozart. Cast: Jean-Paul Belmondo, Jean Seberg, Daniel Boulanger, Henri-Jacques Huet.

Brother Sun, Sister Moon (1973). Production companies: Euro-International, Vic Films, Paramount. Director: Franco Zeffirelli. Screenplay: Suso Cecchi d'Amico, Kenneth Ross, Lina Wertmuller, Franco Zeffirelli. Producer: Luciano Perugia. Cinematography: Ennio Guarnieri. Editors: Reginald Hills, John Rushton. Music: Donovan. Cast: Graham Faulkner, Judi Bowker, Alec Guinness, Leigh Lawson.

Burn (1970). Production company: PEA, United Artists. Director: Gillo Pontecorvo. Screenplay: Franco Solinas, Giorgio Arlorio, based on an original story by Pontecorvo, Solinas and Arlorio. Producer: Alberto Grimaldi. Cinematography: Marcello Goffi. Music: Ennio Morricone. Editors: Enzo Ocone, Mario Morra. Cast: Marlon Brando, Evariste Marquez, Renato Salvatori, Norman Hill.

Bye-Bye Monkey (1978). Production companies: 18 Dicembre, Prospectacle, Action Film. Director: Marco Ferreri. Screenplay: Marco Ferreri, Gérard Brach, Rafael Azcona. Cinematography: Luciano Tavoli. Editor: Ruggero Mastroianni. Music: Philippe Sarde. Cast: Gérard Depardieu, Marcello Mastroianni, James Coco, Gail Lawrence, Geraldine Fitzgerald.

The Canterbury Tales (1972). Production companies: PEA, United Artists. Director: Pier Paulo Pasolini. Screenplay: Pier Paolo Pasolini, after Chaucer. Producer: Alberto Grimaldi. Cinematography: Tonino Delli Colli. Editor: Nino Baragli. Music: English folk songs chosen by Pier Paolo Pasolini and Ennio Morricone. Cast: Pier Paulo Pasolini, Hugh Griffith, Laura Betti, Franco Citti, Ninetto Davoli, Josephine Chaplin.

The Champagne Murders (1967). Production company: Universal. Director: Claude Chabrol. Screenplay: Claude Brule and Derek Prouse from an idea by William Benjamin. Dialogue: Paul Gegauff. Producer: Raymond Eger. Cinematography: Jean Rabier. Editor: Jacques Gaillard. Music: Pierre Jansen. Cast: Anthony Perkins, Maurice Ronet, Stephane Audran, Yvonne Furneaux.

The Coca-Cola Kid (1985). Production companies: Cinecom International, Film Gallery. Director: Dusan Makavejev. Screenplay: Frank Moorhouse. Producer: David Roe. Cinematography: Dean Semler. Editor: John Scott. Music: William Motzing. Cast: Eric Roberts, Greta Scacchi, Bill Kerr.

Confessions of a Holy Drinker (1988). Production companies: Telemax, Aura, Cecchi Gori group, Tiger Cinematografica, RAI1. Director: Ermanno Olmi. Screenplay: Ermanno Olmi, Tullio Kezich, based on a short story by Joseph Roth. Producer: Roberto Cicutto, Vincenzo De Leo. Cinematography: Dante Spinotti. Editors: Ermanno Olmi, Paolo Cottignola. Music: Igor Stravinsky. Cast: Rutger Hauer, Anthony Quayle, Sandrine Dumas.

Contempt (Alternate titles *Le Mépris, Il disprezzo*) (1963). Production companies: Rome-Paris Films, Films Concordia, Compagnia Cinematografica Champion. Director: Jean-Luc Godard. Screenplay: Jean-Luc Godard, based on the novel *Il disprezzo* by Alberto Moravia. Producers: Carlo Ponti, Georges de Beauregard, Joseph E. Levine. Cinematography: Raoul Coutard. Editor: Agnès Guillemot. Music: Georges Delerue (Italian version, Piero Piccioni). Cast: Brigitte Bardot, Michel Piccoli, Jack Palance, Fritz Lang, Georgia Moll.

Conversation Piece (1974). Production companies: Rusconi Films, Gaumont International. Director: Luchino Visconti. Screenplay: Enrico Medioli, Suso Cecchi D'Amico, Luchino Visconti. Producer: Giovanni Bertolucci. Cinematography: Pasqualino de Santis. Editor: Ruggero Mastroianni. Music: Franco Mannino. Cast: Burt Lancaster, Helmut Berger, Silvana Mangano, Claudia Marsani.

Crackers (1984). Production company: Universal. Director: Louis Malle. Screenplay: Jeffrey Fiskin, suggested by the Italian film *Big Deal on Madonna Street*. Producers: Edward Lewis, Robert Cortes. Cinematography: Laszlo Kovacs. Editor: Susanne Baron. Music: Paul Chihara. Cast: Donald Sutherland, Jack Warden, Sean Penn, Wallace Shawn.

Cul de sac (1966). Production company: Compton, Tekli. Director: Roman Polanski. Screenplay: Roman Polanski, Gérard Brach. Producer: Gene Gutowski. Cinematography: Gilbert Taylor. Editor: Alastair McIntyre. Music: Christopher Komeda. Cast: Donald Pleasence, Françoise Dorléac, Lionel Stander, Jack MacGowran, Ian Quarrier.

The Damned (1969). Production companies: Pegaso, Praesidens. Director: Luchino Visconti. Screenplay: Nicola Badalucco, Enrico Medioli, Luchino Visconti. Producers: Alfredo Levy, Ever Haggiag. Cinematography: Armando Nannuzzi, Pasquale de Santis. Editor: Ruggero Mastroianni. Music: Maurice Jarre. Cast: Dirk Bogarde, Ingrid Thulin, Helmut Berger, Helmut Griem, Umberto Orsini, Renaud Verley, Albrecht Schoenhals, Charlotte Rampling.

Death in Venice (1971). Production companies: Alfa Cinematografica, Productions et Editions Cinématographiques Françaises. Director: Luchino Visconti. Screenplay: Luchino Visconti, Nicola Badalucco, from the novella by Thomas Mann. Producers: Mario Gallo, Luchino Visconti, Nicola Badalucco, Robert Gordon Edwards. Cinematography: Pasquale de Santis. Editor: Ruggero Mastroianni. Music: Gustav Mahler, Third and Fifth Symphonies. Cast: Dirk Bogarde, Marisa Berenson, Bjorn Andresen, Silvana Mangano.

Death Watch (1979). Production companies: Selta Films, Little Bear, Antenne 2, Sara Films, Gaumont, SFP-TV13. Director: Bertrand Tavernier. Screenplay: Bertrand Tavernier, David Rayfiel, based on the novel *The Unsleeping Eye* by David Compton. Producers: Gabriel Boustani, Janine Rubeiz. Cinematography: Pierre-William Glenn. Editors: Armand Psenny, Michael Ellis. Music: Antoine Duhamel. Cast: Romy Schneider, Harvey Keitel, Harry Dean Stanton, Thérèse Liotard, Max Von Sydow.

Despair (1978). Production companies: NF Geria II, Sender Freies Berlin, Bavaria Atelier. Director: R. W. Fassbinder. Screenplay: Tom Stoppard, based on a novel by Vladimir Nabokov. Producer: Peter Marthesheimer. Cinematography: Michael Ballhaus. Editor: Reginald Beck. Music: Peer Raben. Cast: Dirk Bogarde, Andrea Ferreol, Volker Spengler, Klaus Lowitsch.

La dolce vita (1960). Production companies: Riama, Pathé Consortium. Director: Federico Fellini. Screenplay: Federico Fellini, Tullio Pinelli, Ennio Flaiano, Brunello Rondi. Producers: Giuseppe Amato, Angelo Rizzoli. Cinematography: Otello Martelli. Editor: Leo Gattozzo. Music: Nino Rota. Cast: Marcello Mastroianni, Anita Ekberg, Anouk Aimée, Alain Cuny, Yvonne Fourneaux, Lex Barker.

The End of the World in Our Usual Bed in a Night Full of Rain (Alternate title: *A Night Full of Rain*) (1978). Production companies: Warner Brothers, Liberty Film. Director: Lina Wertmuller. Screenplay: Lina Wertmuller. Producer: Gil Shiva. Cinematography: Giuseppe Rotunno. Editor: Franco Fraticelli. Music: G. B. Pergolesi, Roberto De Simone. Cast: Giancarlo Giannini, Candice Bergen.

The Empty Canvas (1964). Production company: Embassy. Director: Damiano Damiani. Screenplay: Tonino Guerra, Ugo Liberatore, Damiano Damiani, based on the novel by Alberto Moravia. Producers: Carlo Ponti, Joseph E. Levine. Cinematography: Roberto Gerardi. Editor: Renzo Lucidi. Music: Luis Enriquez Bacalov. Cast: Bette Davis, Horst Buchholz, Catherine Spaak.

Europa 51 (1952). Production company: Ponti/De Laurentiis. Director: Roberto Rossellini. Screenplay: Sandro De Feo, Roberto Rossellini, Mario Pannunzio, Ivo Perilli, Diego Fabbri, Antonio Pietrangeli, Brunello Rondi. Producers: Carlo Ponti, Dino De Laurentiis. Cinematography: Aldo Tonti. Editor: Jolanda Benvenuti. Cast: Ingrid Bergman, Alexander Knox, Sandro Franchina, Ettore Giannini, Giulietta Masina.

Fahrenheit 451 (1965). Production companies: Anglo-Enterprise, Vineyard, Universal. Director: François Truffaut. Screenplay: François Truffaut, Jean-Louis Richard, based on the novel by Ray Bradbury. Additional dialogue: David Rudkin, Helen Scott. Producer: Lewis M. Allen. Cinematography: Nicolas Roeg. Editor: Thom Noble. Music: Bernard Herrmann. Cast: Oskar Werner, Julie Christie, Cyril Cusak, Anton Diffring.

Fellini Casanova (1976). Production companies: PEA, Universal. Director: Federico Fellini. Screenplay: Federico Fellini, Bernardino Zappone, based on *The Memoirs of Casanova*. Producer: Alberto Grimaldi. Cinematography: Giuseppe Rotunno. Editor: Ruggero Mastroianni. Music: Nino Rota.

Cast: Donald Sutherland, Margareth Clementi, Tina Aumont, Cicely Browne, Daniel Berenstein.

Fellini Satyricon (1969). Production companies: PEA, United Artists. Director: Federico Fellini. Screenplay: Federico Fellini and Bernardino Zappone, based on *The Satyricon* by Petronius. Producer: Alberto Grimaldi. Cinematography: Giuseppe Rotunno. Editor: Ruggero Mastroianni. Music: Nino Rota, Ilhan Mimaroglu, Todd Dockstader, Andrew Rudin. Cast: Martin Potter, Hiram Keller, Max Born, Alain Cuny.

The Golden Coach (Alternate title: *Le Carrosse d'or*) (1954). Production companies: Panaria Films, Hoche Productions. Director: Jean Renoir. Screenplay: Jean Renoir, Renzo Avanzo, Giulio Macchi, Jack Kirkland, Ginette Doynel. Freely adapted from the play by Prosper Merimée, "Le Carrosse du Saint-Sacrement." Producer: Francesco Alliata. Cinematography: Claude Renoir and H. Ronald. Editors: Mario Serandrei and David Hawkins. Music: Antonio Vivaldi, adapted by Gino Marinuzzi. Cast: Anna Magnani, Duncan Lamont, Oroardo Spadaro, Riccardo Rioli.

Good Morning, Babylon (1987). Production companies: Filmtre, RAI1, MK2, Films A2, E.P.F.C. Directors: Paolo & Vittorio Taviani. Screenplay: Paolo & Vittorio Taviani. Producers: Giuliani de Negri, Marin Karmitz. Cinematography: Giuseppe Lanci. Editor: Robert Perpignani. Music: Nicola Piovani. Cast: Vincent Spano, Joaquim de Almeida, Greta Scacchi, Desiree Becker.

Hammett (1982). Production companies: Orion Films, Zoetrope Studios. Director: Wim Wenders. Screenplay: Ross Thomas, Dennis O'Flaherty. Executive producer: Francis Ford Coppola. Producers: Fred Roos, Ronald Colby, Don Guest. Cinematography: Philip Lathrop, Joseph Biroc. Editors: Barry Malkin, Mark Laub, Robert Q. Lovett, Wendy Roberts. Music: John Barry. Cast: Frederic Forrest, Peter Boyle, Marilu Henner, Roy Kinnear.

The Handmaid's Tale (1990). Production companies: Bioscop, Cinétudes, Odyssey/Cinecom International. Director: Volker Schlondorff. Screenplay: Harold Pinter, based on the novel by Margaret Atwood. Cinematography: Igor Luther. Editor: David Ray. Music: Ryuichi Sakamoto. Cast: Natasha Richardson, Robert Duvall, Faye Dunaway, Aidan Quinn, Elizabeth McGovern, Victoria Tennant.

Hanna K (1983). Production company: Universal. Director: Costa-Gavras. Screenplay: Franco Solinas. Producer: Costa-Gavras. Cinematography: Ricardo Aronovich. Editor: Françoise Bonnot. Music: Gabriel Yard. Cast: Jill Clayburgh, Jean Yanne, Gabriel Byrne, Mohamed Bakri.

Indiscretions of an American Wife (alternate title *Stazione termini*) (1954). Production company: Selznick. Director: Vittorio de Sica. Screenplay: Cesare Zavattini, Luigi Chiarini, Giorgio Prosperi, Truman Capote. Producers: Vittorio de Sica, David O. Selznick. Cinematography: G. R. Aldo. Editors: Eraldo da Roma, Jean Barker. Music: Aldo Cecognini. Cast: Jennifer Jones, Montgomery Clift, Gino Cervi, Richard Beymer.

I Want to Go Home (1989). Production companies: MK2, La Sept. Director: Alain Resnais. Screenplay: Jules Feiffer. Producer: Marin Karmitz. Cinematography: Charlie Van Damme. Editor: Albert Jurgenson. Music: John Kander. Cast: Gérard Depardieu, Linda Lavin, Adolph Green, Micheline Presle, John Ashton, Geraldine Chaplin.

Julia and Julia (1987). Production company: RAI. Director: Peter del Monte. Screenplay: Silvia Napolitano, Sandro Petraglia, Peter del Monte. Executive Producers: Francesco Pinto, Gaetano Stucchi. Cinematography: Giuseppe Rotunno. Editor: Michael Chandler. Music: Maurice Jarre. Cast: Kathleen Turner, Gabriel Byrne, Sting, Gabriele Ferzetti. Shot in High Definition Video, then transferred to film.

The Last Emperor (1987). Production companies: Yanco Films, Tao Film, Recorded Picture Company. Director: Bernardo Bertolucci. Screenplay: Mark Peploe, Bernardo Bertolucci. Producer: Jeremy Thomas. Cinematography: Vittorio Storaro. Editor: Gabriella Cristiani. Production Design: Ferdinando Scarfiotti. Music: Ryuichi Sakamoto, David Byrne, Cong Su. Cast: John Lone, Joan Chen, Peter O'Toole, Ying Ruocheng, Ryuichi Sakamoto.

Last Tango in Paris (1973). Production companies: PEA, United Artists. Director: Bernardo Bertolucci. Screenplay: Bernardo Bertolucci, Franco Arcalli. Producer: Alberto Grimaldi. Cinematography: Vittorio Storaro. Editor: Franco Arcalli. Music: Gato Barbieri. Cast: Marlon Brando, Maria Schneider, Jean-Pierre Léaud, Maria Michi.

The Leopard (1963). Production companies: Titanus Films, SNPC, SGC, Twentieth Century Fox. Director: Luchino Visconti. Screenplay: Suso Cecchi D'Amico, Enrico Medioli, Pasquale Festa Campanile, Massimo Franciosa, Luchino Visconti, from the novel *Il gattopardo* by Giuseppe Tomasi di Lampedusa. Producer: Goffredo Lombardo. Cinematography: Giuseppe Rotunno. Editor: Mario Serandrei. Music: Nino Rota. Cast: Burt Lancaster, Claudia Cardinale, Alain Delon, Paolo Stoppa.

Lions Love (1969). Production company: Max L. Raab. Director: Agnès Varda. Screenplay: Agnès Varda. Executive producer: Max Raab. Producer: Agnès Varda. Cinematography: Stefan Larner. Editor: Robert Delva. Music:

Joseph Byrd. Cast: Viva, Jerome Ragni, James Rado, Shirley Clarke, Agnès Varda, Eddie Constantine.

Love Is a Funny Thing (1969). Production company: Films 13, United Artists, Films Ariane. Director: Claude Lelouch. Screenplay: Claude Lelouch. Producers: Alexandre Mnouchkine, Georges Dancigers. Cinematography: Jean Collomb, Claude Lelouch. Editor: Claude Barrois. Music: Francis Lai. Cast: Jean-Paul Belmondo, Annie Girardot, Maria-Pia Conte, Marcel Bozzufi, Farah Fawcett. Filmed primarily in the American Southwest.

Lucky Luciano (1974): Production company: Vides, Films la Boétie. Director: Francesco Rosi. Screenplay: Francesco Rosi, Lino Jannuzzi, Tonino Guerra. Producer: Franco Cristaldi. Cinematography: Pasqualino de Santis. Editor: Ruggero Mastroianni. Music: Piero Piccioni. Cast: Gian Maria Volonte, Rod Steiger, Charles Siragusa, Edmund O'Brien, Vincent Gardenia, Charles Cioffi.

Ludwig (1973). Production company: MGM. Director: Luchino Visconti. Screenplay: Luchino Visconti, Enrico Medioli, Suso Cecchi D'Amico. Executive Producer: Robert Gordon Edwards. Producer: Ugo Santalucia. Cinematography: Armando Nannuzzi. Editor: Ruggero Mastroianni. Music: Schumann, Wagner, Offenbach. Cast: Helmut Berger, Romy Schneider, Trevor Howard, Silvana Mangano.

Luna (1979). Production company: Twentieth Century Fox. Director: Bernardo Bertolucci. Screenplay: Giuseppe Bertolucci, Bernardo Bertolucci, Clare Peploe, based on a story by Franco Arcalli, Bernardo Bertolucci, and Giuseppe Bertolucci. Producer: Giovanni Bertolucci. Cinematography: Vittorio Storaro. Editor: Gabriella Cristiani. Music: Mozart, Verdi. Cast: Jill Clayburgh, Matthew Barry, Fred Gwynne, Veronica Lazar, Tomas Milian.

Macbeth (1971). Production companies: Playboy, Columbia. Director: Roman Polanski. Screenplay: Roman Polanski, Kenneth Tynan, based on the play by William Shakespeare. Producer: Andrew Braunsberg. Cinematography: Gil Taylor. Editor: Alastair McIntyre. Music: Third Ear Band. Cast: Jon Finch, Francesca Annis, Martin Shaw, Nicholas Selby.

A Man in Love (1987). Production companies: Camera One, Alexandre Films, J.M.S. Films, Dolly Cinematografica, Cinecom. Director: Diane Kurys. Screenplay: Diane Kurys. Producers: Diane Kurys, Michel Seydoux. Cinematography: Bernard Zitzermann. Editor: Joele Van Effenterre. Music: Georges Delerue. Cast: Peter Coyote, Greta Scacchi, Peter Riegert, John Berry.

Me and Him (1988). Production companies: Neue Constantin, Columbia. Director: Doris Dorrie. Screenplay: Adaptation by Doris Dorrie and Michael Junker, script by Warren D. Leight, based on the novel *Io e lui* by Alberto Moravia. Producer: Bernd Eichinger. Cinematography: Helge Weindler. Editor: Raimund Barthelmes. Music: Klaus Doldinger. Cast: Griffin Dunne, Ellen Greene, Kelly Bishop, Carey Lowell, Craig T. Nelson.

Merry Christmas, Mr. Lawrence (1983). Production company: Recorded Picture Co. Director: Nagisa Oshima. Screenplay: Nagisa Oshima, Paul Mayersberg, based on the novel *The Seed and the Sower* by Laurens van der Post. Producer: Jeremy Thomas. Cinematography: Toichiro Narushima. Editor: Tomoya Oshima. Music: Ryuichi Sakamoto. Cast: David Bowie, Tom Conti, Ryuichi Sakamoto, Takeshi, Jack Thompson.

Missing (1982). Production company: Universal. Director: Costa-Gavras. Screenplay: Costa-Gavras, Donald Stewart from a novel by Thomas Hauser. Producers: Edward Lewis, Mildred Lewis. Cinematography: Ricardo Aronovich. Editor: Françoise Bonnot. Music: Vangelis. Cast: Jack Lemmon, Sissie Spacek, Melanie Mayron, John Sheer.

Model Shop (1969). Production company: Columbia. Director: Jacques Demy. Screenplay: Jacques Demy. Producer: Jacques Demy. Cinematography: Michel Hugo. Editor: Walker Thompson. Music: Spirit, J.S. Bach, Schumann, Rimski-Korsakov. Cast: Gary Lockwood, Anouk Aimée, Alexandra Hay, Carol Cole.

Montenegro (1981). Production companies: Viking Film, Smart Egg Pictures, Europa Film. Director: Dusan Makavejev. Screenplay: Dusan Makavejev. Producer: Bo Jonsson. Cinematography: Tomoslav Pinter. Editor: Sylvia Ingemarsson. Music: Kornell Kovach. Title song sung by Marianne Faithfull. Cast: Susan Anspach, Erland Josephson, Per Oscarsson, John Zacharias.

More (1969). Production companies: Jet Film, Doric Film. Director: Barbet Schroeder. Screenplay: Paul Gegauff, Barbet Schroeder. Producers: Dave Lewis, Charles Lachman. Cinematography: Nestor Almendros. Editor: Denise de Casabianca. Music: Pink Floyd. Cast: Mimsy Farmer, Klaus Grunberg, Heinz Engelmann, Michael Chanderli, Louise Wink.

More than a Miracle (1967). Production companies: Champion, Concordia, MGM. Director: Francesco Rosi. Screenplay: Francesco Rosi, Tonino Guerra, Raffaele La Capria, Peppino Patron. Producer: Carlo Ponti. Cinematography: Pasquale de Santis. Editor: Jolanda Benvenuti. Music: Piero Piccioni. Cast: Sophia Loren, Omar Sharif, Dolores Del Rio, Georgio Wilson, Leslie French.

My Dinner with André (1981). Production company: André Company. Director: Louis Malle. Screenplay: Wallace Shawn, André Gregory. Producers: George W. George, Beverly Karp. Cinematography: Jeri Sopanen. Music: Allen Shawn. Cast: Wallace Shawn, André Gregory.

The Name of the Rose (1986). Production company: Twentieth Century Fox. Director: Jean-Jacques Annaud. Screenplay: Andrew Birkin, Gérard Brach, Howard Franklin, Alain Godard, based on the novel by Umberto Eco. Executive Producers: Thomas Schuckly, Jake Eberts. Producers: Franco Cristaldi, Alexander Mnouchkine. Cinematography: Tonino delli Colli. Editor: Jane Seitz. Music: James Horner. Cast: Sean Connery, F. Murray Abraham, Christian Slater.

Never on Sunday (1960). Production companies: Lopert, Melina Film. Director: Jules Dassin. Screenplay: Jules Dassin. Producer: Jules Dassin. Cinematography: Jacques Natteau. Editor: Roger Dwyer. Music: Manos Hadjidakis. Cast: Melina Mercouri, Jules Dassin, Georges Foundas.

The Night Porter (1974). Production companies: Lotar Films, United Artists. Director: Liliana Cavani. Screenplay: Liliana Cavani, Italo Moscati. Producers: Robert Gordon Edwards, Esa De Simone. Cinematography: Alfio Contini. Editor: Franco Arcalli. Music: Daniele Paris. Cast: Dirk Bogarde, Charlotte Rampling, Philippe Leroy, Gabriele Ferzetti.

1900 (1976). Production companies: PEA, Twentieth Century Fox, Paramount, United Artists. Director: Bernardo Bertolucci. Screenplay: Bernardo Bertolucci, Giuseppe Bertolucci, Franco Arcalli. Producer: Alberto Grimaldi. Cinematography: Vittorio Storaro. Editor: Franco Arcalli. Music: Ennio Morricone. Cast: Gérard Depardieu, Robert De Niro, Sterling Hayden, Burt Lancaster, Dominique Sanda, Stefania Sandrelli, Donald Sutherland, Laura Betti.

One plus One (alternate title *Sympathy for the Devil*) (1968). Production company: Cupid Productions. Director: Jean-Luc Godard. Screenplay: Jean-Luc Godard. Executive Producer: Eleni Collard. Producers: Ian Quarrier, Michael Pierson. Cinematography: Anthony Richmond. Editors: Ken Rowles, Agnès Guillemot. Music: Mick Jagger, Keith Richard. Cast: The Rolling Stones (Mick Jagger, Keith Richard, Brian Jones, Charlie Watts, Bill Wyman), Anne Wiazemsky, Ian Quarrier.

One Woman or Two (1987). Production companies: Hachette-Première, Philippe Dussart, FR 3 Films, DD Production. Director: Daniel Vigne. Screenplay: Daniel Vigne, Elisabeth Rappeneau. Cinematography: Carlo Vanini. Editor: Marie-Josephe Yoyotte. Music: Kevin Mulligan, Evert Vorhees, Toots Thielemans. Cast: Gérard Depardieu, Sigourney Weaver, Dr. Ruth Westheimer.

Paisan (1946). Production companies: OFI, Foreign Film Productions. Director: Roberto Rossellini. Screenplay: Sergio Amidei, Federico Fellini, Roberto Rossellini. Producers: Mario Conti, Rod Geiger. Cinematography: Otello Martelli. Editor: Eraldo da Roma. Music: Renzo Rossellini. Cast:

Carmela Sazio, Robert van Loon, Dots M. Johnson, Alfonsino, Gar Moore, Maria Michi, Harriet White, Renzo Avanzo, Bill Tubbs, Dale Edmunds.

The Palermo Connection (1990). Production companies: Reteitalia, C.G. Silver, Leopard, Gaumont. Director: Francesco Rosi. Screenplay: Francesco Rosi, Gore Vidal, Tonino Guerra, based on a novel by Edmond Charles Roux. Cinematography: Pasqualino De Santis. Editor: Ruggero Mastroianni. Music: Ennio Morricone. Cast: James Belushi, Mimi Rogers, Joss Ackland, Carolina Rosi, Philippe Noiret, Vittorio Gassman.

Paris Does Strange Things (Alternate title *Elena et les hommes*) (1957). Production companies: Franco-London Films, Films Gibé, Electra Compania Cinematografica. Director: Jean Renoir. Screenplay: Jean Renoir, adapted by Jean Renoir and Jean Serge. Producer: Louis Wipf. Cinematography: Claude Renoir. Editor: Boris Lewin. Music: Joseph Kosma; song "Méfiez-Vous de Paris" by Leo Marjane, song "O Nuit" by Juliette Greco; with songs of the period arranged by Georges Van Parys. Cast: Ingrid Bergman, Jean Marais, Mel Ferrer, Jean Richard, Magali Noel, Juliette Greco.

Paris, Texas (1984). Production companies: Road Movies, Argos Films. Director: Wim Wenders. Screenplay: Sam Shepard, adapted by L. M. Kit Carson. Executive Producer: Chris Sievernich. Producer: Don Guest. Cinematography: Robbie Muller. Editor: Peter Przygodda. Music: Ry Cooder. Cast: Harry Dean Stanton, Nastassja Kinski, Dean Stockwell, Hunter Carson, Aurore Clément, Bernhard Wicki.

The Passenger (1975). Production company: MGM. Director: Michelangelo Antonioni. Screenplay: Mark Peploe, Peter Wollen, Michelangelo Antonioni. Producer: Carlo Ponti. Cinematography: Luciano Tovoli. Editors: Franco Arcalli, Michelangelo Antonioni. Cast: Jack Nicholson, Maria Schneider, Jenny Runacre, Ian Hendry.

The Pied Piper (1971). Production companies: Sagittarius, Goodtimes Enterprises, Paramount. Director: Jacques Demy. Screenplay: Andrew Birkin, Jacques Demy, Mark Peploe. Producer: David Puttnam. Cinematography: Peter Suschitsky. Editor: John Trumper. Music: Donovan. Cast: Jack Wild, Donald Pleasence, John Hurt, Donovan.

Pretty Baby (1978). Production company: Paramount. Director: Louis Malle. Screenplay: Polly Platt. Producer: Louis Malle. Cinematography: Sven Nyqvist. Editors: Susanne Baron, Suzanne Fenn. Music: Jerry Wexler, Bob Greene. Cast: Brooke Shields, Susan Sarandon, Keith Carradine.

Providence (1977). Production companies: Action-Films, Société Francaise de Production, FR3, Citel Films. Director: Alain Resnais. Screenplay: David Mercer. Executive Producer: Philippe Dussart. Producers: Yves Gasser, Klaus Hellwig. Cinematography: Ricardo Aronovitch. Editor: Albert Jurgenson. Music: Miklos Rozsa. Cast: John Gielgud, Dirk Bogarde, Ellen Burstyn, David Warner, Elaine Stritch.

Querelle (1983). Production company: Planet. Director: R. W. Fassbinder. Screenplay: Rainer Werner Fassbinder from the book by Jean Genet. Producer: Dieter Schidor. Cinematography: Xaver Schwarzenberger. Editor: Juliane Lorenz. Music: Peer Raben. Cast: Brad Davis, Franco Nero, Jeanne Moreau, Laurent Malet, Nadja Brunkharst.

A Quiet Place in the Country (1968). Production company: PEA, United Artists. Director: Elio Petri. Screenplay: Luciano Vincenzoni, Elio Petri. Producer: Alberto Grimaldi. Cinematography: Luigi Kuveiller. Editor: Juliane Lorenz. Music: Ennio Morricone. Cast: Franco Nero, Vanessa Redgrave, Georges Geret, Madeleine Damien.

Repulsion (1965). Production companies: Compton, Tekli. Director: Roman Polanski. Screenplay: Roman Polanski, Gérard Brach. Producer: Gene Gutowski. Cinematography: Gilbert Taylor. Editor: Alastair McIntyre. Music: Chico Hamilton. Cast: Catherine Deneuve, Ian Hendry, John Fraser, Patrick Wymark, Yvonne Furneaux.

The River (1951). Production company: Oriental International Film. Director: Jean Renoir. Screenplay: Rumer Godden and Jean Renoir, from the novel by Rumer Godden. Producers: Kenneth McEldowney, Kalyan Gupta, Jean Renoir. Cinematography: Claude Renoir. Editor: George Gale. Music: M.A. Parata Sarathy. Cast: Nora Swinburne, Esmond Knight, Arthur Shields, Thomas E. Breen.

Romeo and Juliet (1954). Production company: Rank. Director: Renato Castellani. Screenplay: Renato Castellani, based on the play by William Shakespeare. Producers: Sandro Ghenzi, Joseph Janni. Cinematography: Robert Krasker. Editor: Sidney Hayers. Music: Roman Vlad. Cast: Lawrence Harvey, Susan Shentall, Flora Robson, Mervyn Johns.

Romeo and Juliet (1968). Production companies: B.H.E., Verona Produzione, Dino de Laurentiis, Paramount. Director: Franco Zeffirelli. Screenplay: Franco Brusati, Masolino D'Amico, Franco Zeffirelli, based on the play by William Shakespeare. Producers: Anthony Havelock-Allan, John Brabourne. Cinematography: Pasquale de Santis. Editor: Reginald Mills. Music: Nino Rota. Cast: Leonard Whiting, Olivia Hussey, John McEnery, Michael York. Location scenes filmed in Tuscany.

'Round Midnight (1986). Production company: Warner Brothers. Director: Bertrand Tavernier. Screenplay: David Rayfiel, Bertrand Tavernier. Producer: Irwin Winkler. Cinematography: Bruno de Keyzer. Editor: Armand

Psenny. Music: Herbie Hancock. Cast: Dexter Gordon, François Cluzet, Gabrielle Haker, Sandra Reaves-Phillips.

Sacco and Vanzetti (1971). Production company: Jolly Film. Director: Giuliano Montaldo. Screenplay: Fabrizio Onofri, Giuliano Montaldi. Producers: George Pepi, Harry Colombo. Cinematography: Silvano Ippoliti. Editor: Nino Baragli. Music: Ennio Morricone. Theme ballad lyrics by Joan Baez, sung by Joan Baez. Cast: Gian Maria Volonte, Riccardo Cucciolla, Cyril Cusack.

The Serpent's Egg (1977). Production companies: Rialto, Dino de Laurentiis. Director: Ingmar Bergman. Screenplay: Ingmar Bergman. Producer: Dino de Laurentiis. Cinematography: Sven Nykvist. Editor: Petra van Oelffen. Music: Rolf Wilhelm. Cast: David Carradine, Liv Ullman, Gert Frobe, James Whitmore.

The Sheltering Sky (1990). Production companies: Sahara Co. Ltd., Tao Film SRL, The Aldrich Group. Director: Bernardo Bertolucci. Screenplay: Mark Peploe, Bernardo Bertolucci. Producer: Jeremy Thomas. Cinematography: Vittorio Storaro. Editor: Gabriella Cristiani. Music: Ryuichi Sakamoto, Richard Horowitz. Cast: John Malkovich, Debra Winger, Campbell Scott, Jill Bennett, Timothy Spall, Eric Vu-An.

Spirits of the Dead (1969). Production companies: Films Marceau, Cocinor, PEA. A compilation of short films based on stories by Edgar Allan Poe. "Metzengerstein." Director: Roger Vadim. Cast: Jane Fonda, Peter Fonda. "William Wilson." Director: Louis Malle. Cast: Brigitte Bardot, Alain Cristina. "Toby Dammit." Director: Federico Fellini. Cast: Terence Stamp, Salvo Randone, Marina Yaru.

The State of Things (1983). Production companies: Gray City, Road Movies, V.O. Films. Director: Wim Wenders. Screenplay: Robert Kramer, Wim Wenders. Executive Producer: Chris Sievernich. Cinematography: Henri Alekan and Fred Murphy. Editor: Barbara von Weitershausen. Music: Jurgen Knieper. Cast: Patrick Bauchau, Allen Goorwitz, Isabelle Weingarten, Samuel Fuller.

Stromboli (1949). Production companies: Berit Film, RKO. Director: Roberto Rossellini. Screenplay: Roberto Rossellini. Producer: Roberto Rossellini. Cinematography: Otello Martelli. Editors: Jolanda Benvenuti, Roland Gross. Music: Renzo Rossellini. Cast: Ingrid Bergman, Mario Vitale, Renzo Cesana.

Stroszek (1977). Production companies: Werner Herzog Filmproduktion, Skellig Edition. Director: Werner Herzog. Screenplay: Werner Herzog. Producer: Werner Herzog. Cinematography: Thomas Mauch. Editor: Beate

Mainka-Jellinghaus. Music: Chet Atkins, Sonny Terry. Cast: Bruno S., Eva Mattes, Clemens Scheitz, Wilhelm von Hamburg.

Sweet Movie (1974). Production companies: V.M. Productions, Mojack Films, Maran Films. Director: Dusan Makavejev. Screenplay: Dusan Makavejev. Producers: Vincent Malle, Richard Helman. Cinematography: Pierre L'homme. Editor: Yann Dedel. Music: Manos Hadjidakis. Cast: Carole Laure, Pierre Clémenti, Ann Prucnal, Sami Frey, Jane Mallet.

Tales of Ordinary Madness (1981). Production companies: 23 Giugno, Ginis Film. Director: Marco Ferreri. Screenplay: Sergio Amidei, Marco Ferreri, based on short stories by Charles Bukowski. Producer: Jacqueline Ferreri. Cinematography: Tonino delli Colli. Editor: Ruggero Mastroianni. Music: Philippe Sarde. Cast: Ben Gazzara, Ornella Muti, Susan Tyrrell, Tanya Lopert.

Taming of the Shrew (1967). Production companies: Royal Films International, FAI, Columbia. Director: Franco Zeffirelli. Screenplay: Suso Cecchi d'Amico, Paul Dehn,.Franco Zeffirelli. Producers: Richard McWhorter, Elizabeth Taylor, Richard Burton, Franco Zeffirelli. Cinematography: Oswald Morris. Editor: Peter Taylor. Music: Nino Rota. Cast: Elizabeth Taylor, Richard Burton, Michael York, Michael Hordern.

The Tenant (1976). Production company: Paramount. Director: Roman Polanski. Screenplay: Gérard Brach, Roman Polanski from a novel by Roland Topor. Producer: Andrew Braunsberg. Cinematography: Sven Nykvist. Editor: Françoise Bonnot. Music: Philippe Sarde. Cast: Roman Polanski, Isabelle Adjani, Shelley Winters, Melvyn Douglas.

Ten Days' Wonder (1972). Production company: Films la Boétie. Director: Claude Chabrol. Screenplay: Paul Gardner, Eugene Archer, Paul Gegauff, based on an Ellery Queen novel. Producer: André Genovès. Cinematography: Jean Rabier. Editor: Jacques Gaillard. Music: Pierre Jansen. Cast: Orson Welles, Marlène Jobert, Michel Piccoli, Anthony Perkins.

The 10th Victim (1965). Production companies: CC Champion, Concordia, Embassy. Director: Elio Petri. Screenplay: Tonino Guerra, Giorgio Salvioni, Ennio Flaiano, Elio Petri, based on the story "The Seventh Victim" by Robert Sheckley. Producer: Carlo Ponti. Cinematography: Gianni di Venanzo. Editor: Ruggero Mastroianni. Music: Piero Piccioni. Cast: Marcello Mastroianni, Ursula Andress, Elsa Martinelli, Salvo Randone.

The Touch (1971). Production companies: ABC Pictures, Persona Film. Director: Ingmar Bergman. Screenplay: Ingmar Bergman. Producer: Ingmar Bergman. Cinematography: Sven Nykvist. Editor: Siv Kanalv-Lundgren.

Music: Jan Johansson. Cast: Bibi Andersson, Elliott Gould, Max von Sydow, Sheila Reid.

The Trojan Women (1971). Production company: Josef Shaftel. Director: Michael Cacoyannis. Screenplay: Michael Cacoyannis, based on the play by Euripides. Producers: Michael Cacoyannis, Anis Nohra. Cinematography: Alfio Contini. Editor: Russell Woolnough. Music: Mikis Theodorakis. Cast: Katherine Hepburn, Vanessa Redgrave, Genevieve Bujold, Irene Papas.

Viva Maria (1965). Production companies: Nouvelles Editions, United Artists, Vides. Director: Louis Malle. Screenplay: Louis Malle, Jean-Claude Carrière. Producers: Oscar Dancigers, Louis Malle. Cinematography: Henri Decae. Editors: K. Peltier, Suzanne Baron. Music: Georges Delerue. Cast: Jeanne Moreau, Brigitte Bardot, George Hamilton, Paulette Dubost.

Voyage to Italy (1953). Production company: Sveva, Junior, Italiafilm. Director: Roberto Rossellini. Screenplay: Roberto Rossellini and Vitaliano Brancati. Producer: Roberto Rossellini. Cinematography: Enzo Serafin. Editor: Jolanda Benvenuti. Music: Renzo Rossellini. Cast: Ingrid Bergman, George Sanders, Leslie Daniels, Natalia Ray.

What? (1973). Production company: Avco Embassy. Director: Roman Polanski. Screenplay: Gérard Brach, Roman Polanski. Producer: Carlo Ponti. Cinematography: Marcello Gatti, Giuseppe Ruzzolini. Editor: Alastair McIntyre. Music: Claudio Gizzi. Cast: Marcello Mastroianni, Sydne Rome, Hugh Griffith, Romolo Valli.

Where the Green Ants Dream (1983). Production companies: Werner Herzog Filmproduktion, ZDF. Director: Werner Herzog. Screenplay: Werner Herzog. Producer: Lucki Stipetic. Cinematography: Jorg Schmidt-Reitwein. Editor: Beate Mainka-Jellinghaus. Music: Gabriel Faure, Ernest Bloch, Klaus Jochen-Weis, Richard Wagner, Wandjuk Marika. Cast: Bruce Spence, Roy Marika, Wandjuk Marika, Norman Kaye.

Woman times Seven (1967). Production companies: Twentieth Century Fox, Embassy, Société Nouvelle des Films Cormoran. Director: Vittorio de Sica. Screenplay: Cesare Zavattini. Executive Producer: Joe Levine. Cinematography: Christian Matras. Editors: Teddy Darvas, Victoria Mercanton. Music: Riz Ortolani. Cast: Shirley MacLaine, Peter Sellers, Rossano Brazzi, Vittorio Gassman, Michael Caine, Anita Ekberg.

WR: Mysteries of the Organism (1971). Production companies: Neoplanta Film, Telepol. Director: Dusan Makavejev. Screenplay: Dusan Makavejev. Producer: Svetozar Udovicki. Cinematography: Pega Popovic, Aleksander Petkovic. Editor: Ivanka Vukasovic. Music: Bojana Makavejev. Cast:

Milena Dravic, Jagoda Kaloper, Ivica Vidovic, Tuli Kupferberg, Jackie Curtis. Combines a documentary on the life and ideas of Wilhelm Reich with fictional scenes.

The Young One (1961). Production company: Producciones Olmeca. Director: Luis Buñuel. Screenplay: Luis Buñuel, H.B. Addis, based on the short story "Travellin' Man" by Peter Matthieson. Producer: George P. Werker. Cinematography: Gabriel Figueroa. Editor: Carlos Savage. Music: Jesus Zarzosa. Cast: Zachary Scott, Kay Meersman, Bernie Hamilton, Claudio Brook.

Zabriskie Point (1970). Production company: MGM. Director: Michelangelo Antonioni. Screenplay: Michelangelo Antonioni, Fred Gardner, Sam Shepard, Tonino Guerra, Clare Peploe. Executive Producer: Carlo Ponti. Cinematography: Alfio Contini. Editor: Franco Arcalli. Music: pop songs. Cast: Mark Frechette, Daria Halprin, Rod Taylor, Paul Fix.

Zorba the Greek (1964). Production companies: International Classics 20th Century Fox, Michael Cacoyannis, Rachley. Director: Michael Cacoyannis. Screenplay: Michael Cacoyannis. Producer: Michael Cacoyannis. Cinematography: Walter Lassally. Editor: Michael Cacoyannis. Music: Mikis Theodorakis. Cast: Anthony Quinn, Alan Bates, Irene Pappas, Lila Kedrova.

Bibliography

Adamson, Walter. *Hegemony and Revolution*. Berkeley: University of California Press, 1980.

Andrew, Dudley. *Concepts in Film Theory*. New York: Oxford University Press, 1984.

———. *Film in the Aura of Art*. Princeton: Princeton University Press, 1984.

Antonioni, Michelangelo. *Blow-Up* (script). New York: Simon and Schuster, 1971.

———. "Una intensa emozione che la troupe interrompe." *Cinema Nuovo* 277 (1982): 7–8.

Austin, Bruce. *Immediate Seating: A Look at Movie Audiences*. Belmont, Calif.: Wadsworth, 1988.

Auty, Martin, and Nick Roddick, eds. *British Cinema Now*. London: British Film Institute, 1985.

Balboni, Francesco. "L'esempio italiano." *Bianco e Nero* 35, nos. 9–12 (1974): 160–189.

Balio, Tino. *United Artists: The Company That Changed the Film Industry*. Madison: University of Wisconsin Press, 1987.

Bao Ruo-Wang (Jean Pasqualini), and Rudolph Chelminski. *Prisoner of Mao*. New York: Coward, McCann & Geoghegan, 1973.

Batz, Jean-Claude. *A propos de la crise de l'industrie du cinéma*. Brussels: Université Libre de Bruxelles, 1963.

Behr, Edward. *The Last Emperor*. New York: Bantam, 1987. A biography of Pu Yi written in conjunction with the film by Bertolucci (but not a script or novelization).

Bergman, Ingmar. *The Magic Lantern*. Translated by Joan Tate. New York: Viking, 1988.

Bernstein, Richard. "Is *The Last Emperor* Truth or Propaganda?" *New York Times*, May 8, 1988.

Besas, Peter. *Behind the Spanish Lens*. Denver: Arden, 1985.

Bondanella, Peter. "America and the Post-War Italian Cinema." *Rivista di Studi Italiani* 2 (1984): 106–125.

———. *Italian Cinema*. New York: Ungar, 1983.

Bordwell, David. "The Art Cinema as a Mode of Film Practice." *Film Criticism* 4, no. 1 (1979): 56–64.

————. *Narration in the Fiction Film*. Madison: University of Wisconsin Press, 1985.

————, Janet Staiger, and Kristin Thompson. *The Classical Hollywood Cinema*. New York: Columbia University Press, 1985.

Brunette, Peter. *Roberto Rossellini*. Oxford: Oxford University Press, 1987.

Burgoyne, Robert. "*The Last Emperor*: The Stages of History." *SubStance* 59 (1989): 93–101.

Carrière, Jean-Claude. "Bertolucci à Pékin." *Cahiers du Cinéma* 392 (1987): 6.

Contaldo, Francesco, and Franco Fanelli. *L'affare cinema: Multinazionali produttori e politici nella crisi del cinema italiano*. Milan: Feltrinelli, 1979.

Durgnat, Raymond. *Jean Renoir*. Berkeley: University of California Press, 1974.

"Entretiens à Hollywood: Europe-USA II." *Cinématographe* 66 (special issue), 1981.

"Europe-Hollywood et retour." *Autrement* 79 (complete issue), 1986.

Eidsvik, Charles. *Cineliteracy: Film among the Arts*. New York: Horizon Press, 1978.

Feinstein, Herbert. "An Interview with Jean-Luc Godard." *Film Quarterly* 17, no. 3 (1964): 8–10.

Gambetti, Giacomo. "Per una 'Trilogia populare, libera, erotica.'" *Cineforum* 13, no. 121 (March 1973): 221–229.

Gans, Herbert. "Hollywood Films on British Screens," *Social Problems* 9 (1962). Reprinted in *Literary Taste, Culture and Mass Communication, vol. 5: Literature and Society*, edited by Peter Davison et al., pp. 278–281. New Jersey: Chadwyck-Healey/Somerset, 1978.

Geist, Kathe. *The Cinema of Wim Wenders: From Paris, France to Paris, Texas*. Ann Arbor: UMI Research Press, 1988.

Godard, Jean-Luc. "Contempt." Two unpublished script drafts. Fritz Lang Collection, Department of Special Collections, Doheny Library, University of Southern California, Los Angeles, California.

————. *Introduction à une véritable histoire du cinéma*. Paris: Albatros, 1980.

Gramsci, Antonio. *Selections from Cultural Writings*. Edited by David Forgaes and Geoffrey Nowell-Smith. Translated by William Boelhower. Cambridge, Mass.: Harvard University Press, 1985.

————. *Selections from the Prison Notebooks of Antonio Gramsci*. Edited and translated by Quintin Hoare and Geoffrey Nowell-Smith. New York: International Publishers, 1971.

Greene, Naomi. *Pier Paolo Pasolini: Cinema as Heresy*. Princeton: Princeton University Press, 1990.

Guback, Thomas. "Film and Cultural Pluralism," *Journal of Aesthetic Education* 5, no. 2 (1971): 35–51.

————. "Cultural Identity and Film in the European Economic Community." *Cinema Journal* 14, no. 1 (1974): 2–17.

———. *The International Film Industry*. Bloomington: Indiana University Press, 1969.

Huss, Roy, ed. *Focus on Blow-Up*. New Jersey: Prentice-Hall, 1971.

International Motion Picture Almanac 1989. New York: Quigley, 1989.

Jacobs, Diane. *Hollywood Renaissance*. New Jersey: A.S. Barnes, 1977.

Kagan, Norman. *Greenhorns: Foreign Filmmakers Interpret America*. Ann Arbor: Pierian Press, 1982.

Kané, Pascal. "Cinéma et histoire: L'Effet d'étrangeté." *Cahiers du Cinéma* 254–255 (1974): 77–83.

Kauffmann, Stanley. "The Film Generation: Celebration and Concern." In *A World on Film*, pp. 415–428. New York: Harper & Row, 1966.

Kline, T. Jefferson. *Bertolucci's Dream Loom*. Amherst: University of Massachusetts Press, 1987.

Kolker, Robert. *The Altering Eye*. New York: Oxford University Press, 1983.

———. *Bernardo Bertolucci*. New York: Oxford University Press, 1985.

Lesage, Julia. *Jean-Luc Godard: A Guide to References and Resources*. Boston: G. K. Hall, 1979.

Liehm, Mira. *Passion and Defiance: Film in Italy from 1942 to the Present*. Berkeley: University of California Press, 1984.

MacCabe, Colin. "English Literature in a Global Context." In *English in the World*, edited by Randolph Quirk and H. G. Widdowson, pp. 37–41. Cambridge: Cambridge University Press, 1985.

Mancini, Michele. *Godard*. Rome: Trevi, 1969.

Martini, Emanuela. "Il nostro cinema rischia di tornare a distanze 'coloniali' da quello americano." *Cineforum* 163 (1977): 182–196.

Masson, A. "Halte à l'américanisation!" *Positif* 248 (1981): 2–4.

Mayer, Michael F. *The Film Industries*. 2nd ed. New York: Hastings House, 1978.

———. *Foreign Films on American Screens*. New York: Arco, 1965.

Michalczyk, John J. *The Italian Political Filmmakers*. New Jersey: Fairleigh Dickinson University Press, 1986.

Monaco, James. "Images and Sounds as Cultural Commodities." *Sight and Sound* 49, no. 4 (1980): 229–233.

Monaco, Paul. *Ribbons in Time: Movies and Society since 1945*. Bloomington: Indiana University Press, 1987.

Neale, Steve. "Art Cinema as Institution," *Screen* 22, no. 1 (1981): 11–39.

Nowell-Smith, Geoffrey. "Italy *sotto voce*," *Sight and Sound* 37, no. 3 (1968): 145–147.

Pasolini, Pier Paolo. *Pasolini on Pasolini: Interviews with Oswald Stack*. Bloomington: Indiana University Press, 1969.

———. *Trilogia della vita* (Italian-language scripts for *The Decameron*, *The Canterbury Tales*, and *The Arabian Nights*). Bologna: Cappelli, 1975.

———. "Trilogy of Life Rejected." In *Lutheran Letters*, translated by Stuart Hood, pp. 49–52. New York: Carcanet, 1987.

Perry, Ted, and Rene Prieto. *Michelangelo Antonioni: A Guide to References and Resources*. Boston: G. K. Hall, 1986.

Predal, René. *Le Cinéma français contemporain*. Paris: Editions du Cerf, 1984.

Production Code Administration, Motion Picture Association of America. Files on *Blow-Up* and other films of the 1950s and 1960s. MPAA Collection, Margaret Herrick Library, Academy of Motion Picture Arts and Sciences, Beverly Hills, California.

Pu Yi, Henry. *The Last Manchu*. Edited by Paul Kramer. Translated by Kuo Ying Paul Tsai. New York: Putnam's, 1967.

Ray, Robert B. *A Certain Tendency of the Hollywood Cinema, 1930–1980*. Princeton: Princeton University Press, 1985.

Ryan, Michael, and Douglas Kellner. *Camera Politica*. Bloomington: Indiana University Press, 1988.

Sarris, Andrew. *The American Cinema*. New York: Dutton, 1969.

Schatz, Thomas. *Hollywood Genres*. New York: Random House, 1981.

Serceau, D., and M. Serceau. "Le Mouvement art et essai en France—Quelle signification culturelle et économique?" *Image et Son* 339 (1979): 92–103.

Servadio, Gaia. *Luchino Visconti: A Biography*. New York: Franklin Watts, 1983.

Shepard, Sam. *Motel Chronicles and Hawk Moon*. London: Faber and Faber, 1985.

Siska, William C. "The Art Film." In *Handbook of American Film Genres*, edited by Wes Gehring. Westport, Conn.: Greenwood, 1988.

Smith, Anthony. *The Geopolitics of Information*. New York: Oxford, 1980.

Thompson, Kristin. *Exporting Entertainment: America in the World Film Market 1907–34*. London: British Film Institute, 1985.

Tudor, Andrew. "Death Valley." *Cinema* (London) 6–7 (1970): 23–30.

Tunstall, Jeremy. *The Media Are American*. New York: Columbia University Press, 1977.

Turan, Kenneth, and Stephen Zito. *Sinema*. New York: Praeger, 1974.

United Artists Corporation. Business records of European-made, United Artists-financed films of the 1950s and 1960s. United Artists Collection Addition, Wisconsin Center for Film and Theater Research, Madison, Wisconsin.

Walker, Alexander. *Hollywood UK: The British Film Industry in the Sixties*. New York: Stein and Day, 1974.

Wenders, Wim. *Emotion Pictures: Reflections on the Cinema*. Translated by Sean Whiteside. London: Faber and Faber, 1989.

Willemin, Paul, ed. *Pier Paolo Pasolini*. London: British Film Institute, 1977.

Williams, Raymond. *Keywords*. New York: Oxford University Press, 1986.

———. *Marxism and Literature*. Oxford: Oxford University Press, 1977.

———. *The Sociology of Culture*. New York: Schocken, 1982.

Wyndham, Francis. "The Modelmakers." *London Sunday Times Magazine*, May 10, 1964.

Index